PRIMER

OF

SCIENTIFIC
MANAGEMENT

WITH

AN INTRODUCTION

BY

LOUIS D. BRANDEIS

Elibron Classics
www.elibron.com

PRIMER

OF

SCIENTIFIC
MANAGEMENT

BY

FRANK B. GILBRETH

MEMBER AMERICAN SOCIETY OF MECHANICAL ENGINEERS
CONSULTING MANAGEMENT ENGINEER

WITH AN INTRODUCTION

BY

LOUIS D. BRANDEIS

SECOND EDITION

NEW YORK
D. VAN NOSTRAND COMPANY
25 PARK PLACE
1914

PUBLISHERS' PREFACE

THE publishers of the *American Magazine* printed serially in their issues of March, April, and May, 1911, "The Principles of Scientific Management," by Frederick W. Taylor, M.E., Sc.D.

As a result, hundreds of letters came to them from their readers from all parts of the world, with requests for further information on the subject of the elimination of unnecessary waste in human effort.

These letters were all handed to Mr. Gilbreth to answer the questions they contained, and this book is the result.

The above fact explains, in part at least, why this book is not a complete treatise on Scientific Management.

Mr. Gilbreth's life work has been the elimination of unnecessary waste and fatigue in the operations of human labor. As a follower of Mr. Taylor, he has been able invariably to decrease labor costs and increase wages simultaneously.

The author will welcome any further questions from any interested reader which the present volume does not cover.

TABLE OF CONTENTS

CHAPTER IV

CHAPTER V

FOREWORD

In preparing this Primer of Scientific Management Mr. Gilbreth has performed a public service. His clear and simple instruction in the rudiments of the science will aid managers, superintendents, and foremen in their efforts to introduce it into their business. But the Primer will prove of greatest value in helping to remove from the minds of workingmen misapprehensions which have led some well-meaning labor leaders to oppose a movement from which labor has most to gain. That these labor leaders should, at the outset, have viewed the new management with suspicion was natural and proper. The "Beginning of Wisdom is Fear." But the second step in the path of wisdom is understanding; and courage should not lag far behind.

Scientific Management undertakes to secure greater production for the same or less effort. It secures to the workingman that development and rise in self-respect, that satisfaction with his work which in other lines of human activity accompanies achievement.

Eagerness and interest take the place of indifference, both because the workman is called upon to do the highest work of which he is capable, and also because in doing this better work he secures appropriate and substantial recognition and reward. Under Scientific Management

men are led, not driven. Instead of working unwillingly
for their employer, they work in coöperation with the
management for themselves and their employer on what
is a "square deal." If the fruits of Scientific Management are directed into the proper channels, the workingman will get not only a fair share, but a very large share,
of the industrial profits arising from improved industry.

In order that the workingman may get this large share
of the benefits through higher wages, shorter hours, regular employment, and better working conditions, the labor
unions must welcome, not oppose, the introduction of
Scientific Management to the end that the workingman
through the unions may participate in fixing those wages,
hours, and conditions.

Unless the workingman is so represented, there must be
danger that his interests will not be properly cared for;
and he cannot be properly represented except through
organized labor. The introduction of Scientific Management therefore offers to Organized Labor its greatest
opportunity.

                              LOUIS D. BRANDEIS.

MAY, 1912.

CHAPTER I

DEFINITIONS OF TERMS

Scientific Management

What is scientific management?

Dr. Frederick W. Taylor says: —

"The art of management has been defined 'as knowing exactly what you want men to do and then seeing that they do it in the best and cheapest way' (Shop Management); also, 'The principal object of management should be to secure the maximum prosperity for the employer coupled with the maximum prosperity for each employee.'

"Scientific Management has for its very foundation the firm conviction that the true interests of the two are one and the same; that prosperity for the employer cannot exist through a long term of years unless it is accompanied by prosperity for the employee, and *vice versa;* and that it is possible to give the worker what he most wants — high wages — and the employer what he wants — a low labor cost — for his manufactures."

"Principles of Scientific Management." Harper and Brothers.

Mr. H. K. Hathaway says: —

"For its objects Scientific Management has the saving of energy, materials, and time, or in other words, the elimination of waste, and the increase of the world's wealth resulting from greater productivity of men and machinery. These it aims to achieve, in each industry to which it is applied, through bringing to bear upon each problem the analytical methods of investigation employed in the sciences; developing an art of science with well de-

1

fined and codified laws, in place of uncertain tradition and rule-of-thumb opinion. This is a broad statement of the first principle of Scientific Management."

Mr. James Mapes Dodge says in Paper 1115, Transactions of A. S. M. E., entitled "A History of the Introduction of a System of Shop Management":—

"The Taylor System is not a method of pay, a specific ruling of account books, nor the use of high-speed steel. It is simply an honest, intelligent effort to arrive at the absolute control in every department, to let tabulated and unimpeachable fact take the place of individual opinion; to develop 'team-play' to its highest possibility."

Col. Theodore Roosevelt says:—

"Scientific Management is the application of the conservation principle to production. It does not concern itself with the ownership of our natural resources. But in the factories where it is in force it guards these stores of raw materials from loss and misuse. First, by finding the right material — the special wood or steel or fiber — which is cheapest and best for the purpose. Second, by getting the utmost of finished product out of every pound or bale worked up. We couldn't ask more from a patriotic motive, than Scientific Management gives from a selfish one.

"Now, the time, health, and vitality of our people are as well worth conserving, at least, as our forests, minerals, and lands. And Scientific Management seems to do even more for the workman than for raw materials. It studies him at his task. Of the motions he makes and the efforts he puts forth, it determines by patient observation, which are the ones that get the result. It experiments to see whether these cannot be further shortened, or made easier for him.

"When the right way has been worked out in every detail, Scientific Management sets it up as a standard for that job; then instructs and trains the workman until he can accomplish this standard. And so on with all other workmen and all other jobs. The individual is first made efficient; his productive capacity is raised twenty-five or fifty per cent, sometimes doubled. From these efficient units is built up an efficiency organization. And when we get efficiency in all our industries and commercial ventures, national efficiency will be a fact."

Mr. Brandeis says in "Scientific Management and the Railroads," published by *Engineering Magazine*, New York: —

"Scientific Management means universal preparedness, the same kind of preparedness that secured to Prussia a victory over France and to Japan a victory over Russia. In Scientific Management nothing is left to chance; all is carefully planned in advance.

"Every operation is to be performed according to a predetermined schedule under definite instructions; and the execution under the plan is inspected and supervised at every point. Errors are prevented instead of being corrected. The terrible waste of delays and accidents is avoided. Calculation is substituted for guess; demonstration for opinion. The high efficiency of the limited passenger train is sought to be obtained in the ordinary operations of the business."

Professor Roe of Yale says that "Scientific Management" consists of three things: —

1. Accurate determination of the method and time in which a piece of work should be done.
2. Detailed instructions for 1.
3. Rewards and penalties to secure 1 and 2.

Mr. Cleveland Moffat says: —

"The basis of Scientific Management, as it is of art, is the rigorous cutting away of superfluities — not one wasted motion, not one wasted minute."

Engineering and Contracting says, in an editorial in the April 5, 1911, issue : —

"As we conceive it, Scientific Management consists in the conscious application of the laws inherent in the practice of successful managers and the laws of science in general. It has been called management engineering, which seems more fully to cover its general scope of the science."

Mr. Arthur W. Page says on page 14049 of *World's Work:* —

"What is 'Scientific Management'?

" Many people get the impression that Scientific Management consists of slide rules, instruction cards, eight sets of shovels, and the like.

" In reality the appliances are the least important part of it. The main thing is, first, to get the accurate information and, second, to continuously apply it."

Mr. H. L. Gantt says: —

" A system of management, to deserve the term 'scientific,' should aim to meet the following four conditions: —

"1. It should provide means for utilizing all of the available knowledge concerning the work in hand.

" 2. It should provide means for seeing that the knowledge furnished is properly utilized.

"3. It should award liberal compensation for those who do use it properly.

"4. It should provide liberal means for acquiring new knowledge by scientific investigation, with adequate rewards for success.

"In introducing such a system, my advice is to begin at the bottom and go slowly."

W. B. Laine says: —

"Scientific Management is that form of Management which —

"(1) Separates an operation into its elements and determines — by study, observation, and experiment of unit times and motions — standards of equipment and method with definite instructions for operation; and

"(2) Determines a definite task difficult of attainment, but possible of daily and continuous performance with conservation of the physical and mental health of the worker; and

"(3) Routes material and effort in accordance with determined standards, providing instruction by functionally operating and trained teachers for the worker; and

"(4) Determines methods of payment, assuring a wage considerably above the ordinary and giving a large reward for attainment of the task and a definite loss for failure; and

"(5) By the elimination of waste material and effort, lost time, idle machinery, and capital, assures the maximum of prosperity for the employer and the employee."

TAYLOR SYSTEM

What is the difference between Scientific Management and the Taylor Plan?

Dr. Taylor's functional foreman plan of management founded upon time study is the *basis* for all scientific management, *i.e.* for types of management where scientific laboratory methods of analysis are substituted for the rule of "thumb methods" that have been handed down by word of mouth.

The Taylor plan of management is generally known as "Scientific Management," although there are many plans of management formulated by scientists that do not conform to the laws of management as discovered by Dr. Taylor.

Why is not Scientific Management called " the Taylor System " ?

That type of management founded upon the best recognized scientific principles of to-day *should* be known as Taylor's plan of management, and *would* be, but for the personal objections of Dr. Taylor.

Where is Scientific Management best explained?

Dr. Taylor's writings describe his work in full.   See:—

Transactions of the American Society of Mechanical Engineers, Papers numbered —
647. —"A Piece Rate System."   June, 1895.
1003. —"Shop Management."   June, 1903.
1119. —"On the Art of Cutting Metals."   December, 1906.

Also

American Magazine — March, April, May, 1911.
" The Principles of Scientific Management."   Harper's.
" Shop Management."   Harper's.

The value of Dr. Taylor's work was appreciated very early.

Mr. Harrington Emerson, industrial engineer, recognized the epoch-making value of A. S. M. E. Paper 1003 at the time of its presentation before the American Society of Mechanical Engineers, in 1903, when he said: —

"I regard the paper presented at this meeting by Mr. Taylor as the most important contribution ever presented to the Society, and one of the most important papers ever published in the United States."

TIME STUDY

What is " Time Study " ?

Time study is the art of recording, analyzing, and synthesizing the time of the elements of any operation, usually a manual operation, but it has also been extended to mental and machinery operations.

It is one of the many remarkable inventions of Dr. Taylor while he was working at the Midvale Steel Works. It differs from the well-known process of timing the complete operation, as, for instance, the usual method for timing the athlete, in that the timing of time study is done on the elements of the process. Much ridiculous criticism has been put forward by well-meaning but uninformed persons, who claim that timing a worker down to a three hundredth of a minute is unkind, inhuman, and conducive to the worst form of slavery ever known. On the contrary, obtaining precise information regarding the smallest elements into which an art or a trade can be subdivided, and examining them separately, is the method adopted in all branches of scientific research.

For description of time study data by Mr. Sanford E. Thompson, C. E., see "Shop Management," Harper and Brothers.

For time study by Mr. R. T. Dana, see "Handbook of Steam Shovel Work," The Bucyrus Co.

MOTION STUDY

What is Motion Study?

Motion study is the science of eliminating wastefulness resulting from using unnecessary, ill-directed, and inefficient motions.

The aim of motion study is to find and perpetuate the scheme of least waste methods of labor.

By its use we have revolutionized several of the trades.[1] There is probably no art or trade that cannot have its output doubled by the application of the principles of motion study.   Among the variables affecting the motions most, are

VARIABLES OF THE WORKER

Anatomy	Experience	Nutrition
Brawn	Fatigue	Size
Contentment	Habits	Skill
Creed	Health	Temperament
Earning power	Mode of living	Training

VARIABLES OF THE SURROUNDINGS, EQUIPMENT, AND TOOLS

Appliances	Reward and punishment
Clothes	Size of unit moved
Colors	Special fatigue eliminating
Entertainment, music, reading, etc.	devices
	Surroundings
Heating, cooling, ventilating	Tools
Lighting	Union rules
Quality of material	Weight of unit moved

[1] "Motion Study," published by D. Van Nostrand Company, 25 Park Place, New York.

VARIABLES OF THE MOTION

Acceleration
Automaticity
Combination with other motions and sequence
Cost
Direction
Effectiveness
Foot pounds of work accomplished
Inertia and momentum overcome
Length
Necessity
Path
Play for position
Speed

Arthur Twining Hadley, President of Yale University, states in his book "Economics" : —

"The ability of a community to pay high wages seems to depend more upon the avoidance of waste than upon increase of accumulations."

TASK

What is meant by the word "task"?

The quantity of work of prescribed quality to be done in a given time, or the time required to do a certain quantity of output in a certain way as prophesied by scientific time study, is called the "task." The task is determined by building up synthetically the easiest, least fatiguing, least wasteful method, and allowing a definite percentage of time for rest, and a definite percentage for unavoidable delays. This percentage seldom amounts to less than 12½ per cent and often reaches to more than 30 per cent, and in some cases over 50 per cent.

The task is obviously, then, not a measure of how much a man can do under a short burst of speed, but instead is that maximum quantity that he can do day after day without speeding up and year after year with improvement to his health.

The task is the quantity that the man who is actually to do the work can do continuously and thrive.

FUNCTIONAL FOREMEN

What is the meaning of "Functional Foremen"?

Functional foremen differ from the usual type of foremen in that, while the latter have full charge of a certain number of men, the former have charge of a certain function in the handling of the men. For example, the principal functional foremen under the Taylor plan consist of

(a) Route clerk, and order of work clerk.
(b) Instruction card clerk.
(c) Time and cost clerk.
(d) Disciplinarian.
(e) Gang boss.
(f) Speed boss.
(g) Repair boss.
(h) Inspector.

All of these functional foremen must be specialists at their functions and must be prepared constantly to teach and help the individual workman with whom they work in direct contact.

The functional foreman under the scientific plan of management differs from the foreman under the traditional plan of management in that the latter has so many functions and duties to perform that he has to depend largely upon the individual workman to guess for himself as to which is the best way to do the work and to hold his job.

Regarding the savings and economic benefits accruing from the general principle of division of labor, Adam Smith said in 1776 ("An Inquiry into the Nature and Causes of the Wealth of Nations") : —

"This great increase in the quantity of work, which, in consequence of the division of labor, the same number of people are capable of performing, is owing to three different circumstances: first, to the increase of dexterity in every particular workman; secondly, to the saving of time which is commonly lost in passing from one species of work to another; and, lastly, to the invention of a great number of machines which facilitate and abridge labor, and enable one man to do the work of many."

Regarding division of mental labor, Charles Babbage said:—

"The effect of the *division of labor*, both mechanical and in mental operations, is, that it enables us to purchase and apply to each process precisely that quantity of skill and knowledge which is required for it; we avoid employing any part of the time of a man who can get eight or ten shillings a day by his skill in tempering needles, in turning a wheel, which can be done for sixpence a day; and we equally avoid the loss arising from an accomplished mathematician in performing the lowest processes of arithmetic."

CHAPTER II

LAWS OR PRINCIPLES OF SCIENTIFIC MANAGEMENT

TIME STUDY

What is the fundamental of Scientific Management?

The great fundamental of Scientific Management is time study.

On time study hangs the entire plan of the Taylor system of management. The apparently simple art of time study is in reality a great invention, for, previous to Taylor's discovery of it, there was no practical way of predetermining or prophesying accurately the amount of work that a man could do before he actually commenced to do it.

Any plan of management that does not include Taylor's plan of time study cannot be considered as highly efficient. We have never seen a case in our work where time study and analysis did not result in more than doubling the output of the worker. The greatest need to-day, as Dr. Taylor has already pointed out, is a hand-book of time study data for assisting the workers to earn higher wages and the management to secure lower production costs. It is hoped that the day will soon arrive when the colleges will coöperate in undertaking this work in accordance with a definite plan, with a national bureau in charge of the entire work.

What are the purposes of Time Study?

The purposes of the scientific study of unit times are five, as follows: —

1. To obtain all the existing information about the art or trade being investigated that is possessed by the present masters, journeymen, and experts of that trade, who obtained the most of their information through the "journeyman to apprentice method" of teaching.

2. To get the most exact information regarding the time required to perform each smallest element of the operation, so that in building up the standard method synthetically the quickest elements and motions may be selected, in order that the workman can, other things being equal, use a method consisting of elements requiring the least time to perform.

3. To determine which motions and elements are the least fatiguing, that the worker may be caused no unnecessary fatigue in his work, nor any fatigue outside of his work of actually producing output.

4. To determine the amount of actual rest that each kind of work requires, that neither the management nor the man himself may injure the man by trying to make him do too much in order to obtain an increase over and above the unusually high wages offered by Scientific Management.

5. To determine the personal coefficient of each applicant for certain kinds of work, that he may be assisted in entering that vocation for which he is best fitted.

It will be seen by the above that it is necessary to obtain the most accurate and minute times if the greatest good to the worker and the management is to be obtained.

Why is the establishment of standards of tools, methods, and devices of such vital importance as a preliminary?

This is best answered by Mr. Morris Llewellyn Cooke, in his valuable "Report to the Carnegie Foundation For the Advancement of Teaching." He says (p. 6) : —

"A standard under modern Scientific Management is simply a carefully thought out method of performing a function, or carefully drawn specification covering an implement or some article of stores or of product. The idea of perfection is not involved in standardization. The standard method of doing anything is simply the best method that can be devised at the time the standard is drawn. Improvements in standards are wanted and adopted whenever and wherever they are found. There is absolutely nothing in standardization to preclude innovation. But to protect standards from changes which are not in the nature of improvements, certain safeguards are erected. These safeguards protect standards from change for the sake of change. All that is demanded under modern scientific management is that a proposed change in a standard must be scrutinized as carefully as the standard was scrutinized prior to its adoption ; and further that this work be done by experts as competent to do it as were those who originally framed the standard. Standards adopted and protected in this way produce the best that is known at any one time. Standardization practiced in this way is a constant invitation to experimentation and improvement."

In what way can the general adoption of standards save money?

Dr. Taylor in his Paper 1003 ("Shop Management"), American Society of Mechanical Engineers, says : —

"284. It would seem almost unnecessary to dwell upon the desirability of standardizing, not only all of the tools, appliances, and implements throughout the works and office, but also the methods to be used in the multitude of small operations which are repeated day after day. There are many good managers of the old school, however, who feel that this standardization is not only unnecessary, but that it is undesirable, their principal reason being that it is better to allow each workman to develop his individuality by choosing the particular implements and methods which suit him best. And there is considerable weight in this contention when the scheme of management is to allow each workman to do the work as he pleases and hold him responsible for results. Unfortunately, in ninety-nine out of a hundred such cases only the first part of this plan is carried out. The workman chooses his own methods and implements, but is NOT HELD IN ANY STRICT SENSE ACCOUNTABLE unless the quality of the work is so poor or the quantity turned out is so small as to almost amount to a scandal. In the type of management advocated by the writer, this complete standardization of all details and methods is not only desirable, but absolutely indispensable as a preliminary to specifying the time in which each operation shall be done, and then insisting that it shall be done within the time allowed.

"285. Neglecting to take the time and trouble to thoroughly standardize all of such methods and details is one of the chief causes for setbacks and failure in introducing this system. Much better results can be attained, even if poor standards be adopted, than can be reached if some of a given class of implements are the best of their kind while others are poor. It is uniformity that is required. Better have them uniformly second class than mainly first with some second and some third class thrown in at random. In the latter case the workmen will almost always adopt the pace which conforms to the third class instead of the first or second. In fact, however, it is not a matter involving any great expense or time to select in each case standard implements which shall be nearly the best or the best of their kinds. The writer has never failed to make enormous gains in the economy of running by the adoption of standards.

"286. It was in the course of making a series of experiments with various air hardening tool steels with a view to adopting a standard for the Bethlehem works that Mr. White, together with the writer, discovered the Taylor-White process of treating tool steel, which marks a distinct improvement in the art; and the fact that this improvement was made, not by manufacturers of tool steel, but in the course of the adoption of standards, shows both the necessity and fruitfulness of methodical and careful investigation in the choice of much neglected details. The economy to be gained through the adoption of uniform standards is hardly realized at all by the managers of this country. No better illustration of this fact is needed than that of the present condition of the cutting tools used throughout the machine shops of the United States. Hardly a shop can be found in which tools made from a dozen different qualities of steel are not used side by side, in many cases with little or no means of telling one make from another; and, in addition, the shape of the cutting edge of the tool is in most cases left to the fancy of each individual workman. When one realizes that the cutting speed of the best treated air hardening steel is for a given depth of cut, feed, and quality of metal being cut, say sixty feet per minute, while with the same shaped tool made from the best carbon tool steel and with the same conditions, the cutting speed will be only twelve feet per minute, it becomes apparent how little the necessity for rigid standards is appreciated."

How can instruction cards be made out for laborers who cannot write or read any language, and who also cannot speak or understand the language of the management?

There are several ways of overcoming this difficulty. If the job is a long one of highly repetitive work, it is sometimes advisable to get an interpreter who can translate and teach the instruction card to the men. If the men read, it is possible to print the entire card in the two languages.

Where this has not been advisable, we have found that a full-sized exhibit of a complete unit to be constructed, maintained in all its various stages, and shown in detail as to method and result, has contained enough of the principles and features of the instruction card to serve the purpose.

We have found that stereoscopic (3-dimension) photographs and a stereoscope have been a great help, not only where the men do not understand the language of the management, but also in cases where they do.

Dr. Taylor says : —

"The instruction card can be put to wide and varied use. It is to the art of management what the drawing is to engineering, and, like the latter, should vary in size and form according to the amount and variety of the information which it is to convey. In some cases it should consist of a pencil memorandum on a small piece of paper which will be sent directly to the man requiring the instructions, while in others it will be in the form of several pages of typewritten matter, properly varnished and mounted, and issued under the check or other record system, so that it can be used time after time."

And any method or device that will enable the management to explain to the men exactly what is wanted, that they may do the performing exactly in accordance with the method required by the planning department, will perform the functions of the instruction card.

In whatever form or physical shape the instrument for conveying the information from the planning department is, one thing is certain, *i.e.* that the more explicit and definite this information, the better the results will be.

FUNCTIONAL FOREMEN

With so many functional foremen, who shall decide when they disagree?

Each functional foreman decides matters pertaining to his own work. In case of a disagreement, the disciplinarian decides as to questions of discipline and penalties.

On large works, where there are several foremen working at the same function, if they cannot agree immediately, the decision is left to their respective overforemen. If these, in turn, disagree, the question is referred to the assistant superintendent.

What is the advantage of a disciplinarian over a self-governing body?

The disciplinarian should be a trained specialist, who holds his job during good and efficient behavior. He should be free from the politics of election by a self-governing body. He should also be " of the management " in selecting employees, fixing base rates of wages, and determining promotion of deserving workers and foremen.

Don't the foremen have to spend too much of their time looking at papers instead of pushing the men?

The foremen in the planning department put their orders and teachings in writing on paper, defining clearly the standard method of doing the work.

The foremen of the performing department do not drive the men. Their duties are to explain the written orders of the planning department, and to see that they are carried out exactly as written.

Inasmuch as the papers show and describe the best-known method, it is essential that the foremen follow the instructions on the instruction card to the letter in order to obtain the best results.

How can a worker serve eight masters?

These eight so-called "masters" are functional foremen whose duties are to help the worker to do his work in the exact manner called for on the instruction card. Each man thus belongs to eight different gangs, or classes of instruction, and receives help from all eight teachers. "A man cannot serve two masters," but he can easily receive and accept help from eight teachers.

Mr. Wilfred Lewis, President of the Tabor Manufacturing Company, stated recently in an address on Scientific Management at the Congress of Technology, Boston, April ·10, 1911, speaking of his own experience with the Taylor System: —

" Our wonderful increase in production is not due entirely to rapidity of performance, for in some instances very little gain in that direction has been made. A great deal is due to the functional foreman, whose duty it is to prepare and guide the way of every piece of work going through the shop.

" The old notion that a man cannot serve two masters or take orders from more than one superior is denied by the new philosophy, which makes it possible for a workman to have as many bosses as there are functions to be performed. There is no conflict of authority unless the functions overlap, and even there such conflict as may arise is salutary and to the interest of the company."

RATE OF COMPENSATION

How is it possible to pay high wages and at the same time have low costs of labor?

By finding the best way to do the work. This will enable the worker to produce much higher records of output at a lower unit cost, yet at a higher total daily wage, than he received under the old form of management. For example, suppose that under the old plan of management a man turned out about 10 pieces per day and received a total daily wage of $4.00. That would equal forty cents apiece.

Now suppose that by analyzing the method of making, down to the minutest motions, and by discovering a new method that took less time with less effort and was subject to less delay, the worker was able to put out 25 pieces, for which he received twenty-five cents apiece. The man's pay is here raised more than 56 per cent, and the production costs have been lowered $37\frac{1}{2}$ per cent, out of which must be paid the cost of the investigation and of the planning department.

What are the essential differences between the different methods of payment and what are the good points and the failings of each?

(a) *Day Work.* — The most common method of payment of the worker, especially in establishments where but few men are employed, is the day work plan. Under this plan a man is paid for the time he works, and there is no agreement as to how much work he shall do in order to earn his day's pay.

Theoretically, this plan is very good, but in practice it is a great factor in decreasing efficiency, raising costs, reducing outputs, and, eventually, decreasing wages.

The day work system of payment would be an ideal method of payment of the workmen, from both the standpoint of the workers and the employers, if the employers could tell what rate per day would be the correct amount to pay each workman. But there is no way of determining that easily, consequently the men are paid by the position they hold and not for their individual merit, skill, or productivity. The workmen, seeing that their pay is determined by their class of trade, immediately recognize that it is useless to be particularly efficient because it will not affect their pay in the long run. Consequently all hands soon fall into that easy-going pace that is just fast enough to hold their job.

(b) *Old Bonus Scheme.* — The old scheme of paying a bonus has grown into disfavor generally because under it the amount of bonus was not determined scientifically; and, finally, it was used as a club over the heads of the workmen to drive them to greater efforts without adequate or just financial rewards. It also resulted in a poorer quality of finished output and oftentimes in accidents and injuries due to the generally careless methods resulting from the incentive to earn the extra financial reward.

(c) *Old-fashioned Piecework.* — Piecework would be an ideal method for paying the men if it were not for several facts not readily recognized as being of great injustice to the worker. First comes the difficulty of finding out the correct and just price that should be paid per piece.

Then there is the injustice to the worker while he is learning to do the work, also the fear on the part of the worker that the employer will cut the rate if he earns what the employer thinks is too much. Finally comes systematic soldiering, which is the worst thing in any type of management.

(d) *Gain Sharing.* — This method of compensating the workman was invented by Mr. Henry R. Towne in 1886. This method is fully described in the Transactions of the American Society of Mechanical Engineers, 1889, Paper 341.

(e) *Premium Plan.* — This method of paying workmen was invented by Mr. F. A. Halsey and is fully described in the Transactions of the American Society of Mechanical Engineers, 1891, Paper 499.

Mr. Taylor discusses these two methods of management (see Transactions of the American Society of Mechanical Engineers, 1895, Paper 647, ¶¶ 27–30).

(f) *Task with Bonus.* — This system was invented by Mr. H. L. Gantt. It consists of paying a regular day's pay to the worker in every case, even while he is learning and is unable to produce much output. It also provides for a scientifically determined task of standard quality, for the accomplishment of which the worker receives from 30 to 100 per cent extra wages. For any excess of output over and above the quantity of the task, the worker is paid at the same piece rate as is the rate a piece for the task. This is, therefore, a simple yet remarkable invention, for it insures a minimum of a full day's pay for the unskilled and the learners, and piecework for the skilled. (See "Work, Wages, and Profits," published by *The Engineering*

Magazine. See also Paper 928, Transactions of the American Society of Mechanical Engineers.)

(*g*) *Three-rate with Increased Rate.* — This system has many advantages in certain cases, and we have found it to be extremely valuable during the period of teaching the workmen how to achieve the task. It consists of —

(1) Paying a usual and customary day's pay to every worker, called the low rate.

(2) Paying a day's pay plus 10 per cent to a worker when he conforms to the exact method described upon the instruction card. This is called the middle rate and is used for the purpose of encouraging the worker and of inducing him to conform with great exactness to that method on which the unit times for work and percentage of time allowed for rest and unavoidable delays are based, and which has been determined by the planning department to be the best method that they have seen, heard of, or been able to devise by making a one best way from uniting best portions of many workers' methods. This middle rate is abandoned as soon as the worker has once achieved the task in the standard method. For the accomplishment of the task, which has been derived by scientific time study, an extra payment of from 30 to 100 per cent above the low rate. This is called the high rate, and for anything above the task a wage equal to the same piece rate for the increased quantity is paid. In some cases it is advisable to pay an increasing or differential rate for each piece when the number of pieces exceeds that of the task.

(*h*) *Differential Rate Piece.* — The Differential Rate Piece is an invention of Mr. Taylor, and, like everything he has done, is the most efficient of all methods of payment.

This method is undoubtedly the best method of compensating the worker. It gives unusually high pay for high outputs and unusually low pay for low outputs. It rewards the man who conforms to his instruction card so that he is most particular to coöperate with the management for the complete achievement of his task.

Paying an unusually low piece rate for failure to make obtainable output seems like a hardship on the worker; but it is absolutely necessary to penalize the lazy in this way because the "dependent sequences," as Mr. Harrington Emerson has described them, make it necessary to induce all men to work, by means of high pay for successful effort and low pay for lack of effort. In this way one worker, or class of workers, is not absolutely prevented from doing its work, which is dependent upon the preceding condition that the first workers achieve their tasks.

Example. — A bricklayer cannot achieve his task unless he is supplied with the brick, mortar, scaffold, and "line up" in the correct sequence at the right time, the right quantity, and of the right quality.

The mortar men cannot transport the mortar until it has been mixed. The mortar cannot be mixed until its ingredients have been received, etc.

While the Differential Rate Piece system is the most efficient, it should not be used until all the accompanying conditions for its success, including time study, the task, provision for proper inspection, methods and tools generally have been perfected and standardized.

While it is the most efficient, it requires a higher standard of management before it can be used to best advantage. It is particularly efficient on work that is repeated day after day and year after year.

It is hardly to be expected that any large establishment will ever have all employees working under one system of payment, therefore the system of payment must be selected according to the general condition of the management, whether or not work is sufficiently repetitive to warrant making entirely new time studies and instruction cards and many other factors controlling the situation.

Different methods of compensating workmen are explained particularly well in Chapter III of "Cost Keeping and Management Engineering," by Gillette and Dana.

It is necessary to say, further, that many ill-prepared antagonists to Scientific Management have stated frankly that they were "against any kind of a bonus scheme." It must be remembered, however, that "the method of payment is no more Scientific Management than a shingle is a roof," as Mr. Ernest Hamlin Abbott has so aptly stated.

Will not the use of different systems of payment make all kinds of confusion in an establishment?

No, on the contrary, the different conditions governing the work make it necessary to use several different forms of compensation to the workmen in order to secure the best results. In fact, the existence of a class of work on which the men are paid by the day provides one of the best forms of punishment for the use of the disciplin-

arian.   After the men have gotten the high wages resulting from following the teachings provided for them,
they dislike exceedingly to be put into the "day's pay"
class.   In the Link-Belt Co.'s works, — which are conceded
to be of the most highly systematized, — there are at least
four systems of payment, namely: —

(a) Day work,
(b) Piecework,
(c) Task with Bonus, and
(d) Differential Rate Piece.

The same is true with the Tabor Manufacturing Co.,
the Brighton Mills, Plimpton Press, Yale and Towne
Manufacturing Co., and several works under the able
management of Messrs. Dodge, Day and Zimmerman.

**Why is not a coöperative plan better than Taylor's
plan?**

This question is best answered by quoting from Dr.
Taylor's paper read before the A. S. M. E. in 1895, entitled
a "Piece Rate System."   We quote also pp. 73 to 77 in-
clusive of American Society of Mechanical Engineers,
Paper 1003.

"73. Coöperation, or profit sharing, has entered the
mind of every student of the subject as one of the possible and most attractive solutions of the problem; and
there have been certain instances, both in England and
France, of at least a partial success of coöperative experiments.

"74. So far as I know, however, these trials have been
made either in small towns, remote from the manufacturing centers, or in industries which in many respects
are not subject to ordinary manufacturing conditions.

" 75. Coöperative experiments have failed, and, I think, are generally destined to fail, for several reasons, the first and most important of which is, that no form of coöperation has yet been devised in which each individual is allowed free scope for his personal ambition. Personal ambition always has been and will remain a more powerful incentive to exertion than a desire for the general welfare. The few misplaced drones, who do the loafing and share equally in the profits with the rest, under coöperation are sure to drag the better men down toward their level.

" 76. The second and almost equally strong reason for failure lies in the remoteness of the reward. The average workman (I don't say all men) cannot look forward to a profit which is six months or a year away. The nice time which they are sure to have to-day, if they take things easily, proves more attractive than hard work, with a possible reward to be shared with others six months later.

" 77. Other and formidable difficulties in the path of coöperation are the equitable division of the profits, and the fact that, while workmen are always ready to share the profits, they are neither able nor willing to share the losses. Further than this, in many cases, it is neither right nor just that they should share either in the profits or the losses, since these may be due in great part to causes entirely beyond their influence or control, and to which they do not contribute."

Isn't it really the old piecework scheme under a new name with a few frills added?

In its final analysis, all compensation is more or less piecework. Even "day work" is a kind of piecework, *i.e.* the employer in effect says "I'll give you so much per day." Then if he thinks that he is not getting enough pieces done for the money, perhaps he does not say anything more, but simply sends the blue envelope to the worker.

Another employer might say, "I'll pay you 25 cents apiece," he and the employee both thinking that the latter could make anywhere from 8 to 16 pieces per day. There is one great objection to this method that does not always show up immediately. When it does, it does more damage than enough to offset all its value; namely, when, by special effort on the part of the employee, he makes say 32 pieces per day, and the employer, knowing that there are plenty of men to be had who would be delighted to work for $2.00 to $4.00 per day, cuts the rate. As Dr. Taylor says, just two cuts of the rate for the same man, and he will then stop all planning except on the subject of how much output he can safely make without the fear of another cut. It is surely not for the employee's interest to make any extra effort unless he is to be compensated for it. This necessitates the setting of the piece rate scientifically and not by guess or arbitration or collective bargainings, and we say this emphatically, although we are thoroughly in favor of collective bargaining on many things, such, for example, as the minimum day's rate to be paid to the worker and the number of hours in the working day.

We will digress for a moment here and tell of an incident seen some years ago. We had occasion to visit a factory, and saw a girl putting four-ounce lots of the factory's product into pasteboard boxes. Her duties were simply to put exactly four ounces of merchandise into each pasteboard box and to put the cover on. She was doing her work in a most inefficient way — obviously so.

Knowing that all the employees in that factory were on

piecework, we suggested to this girl that we could show her some economies of motions that would increase her output. She seemed much interested and watched our stop watch record an output several times greater our way than the way she had been working. She seemed delighted with the suggestion, and we were pleased to have shown her how she could do so many more dozen boxes per day. She followed the suggestion for about ten minutes, or until we walked away. When we came back, we saw that she was doing her work in the old way. We asked her why she did not do the work our way when it was so much more efficient. Her discouraged reply was, "What's the use; the boss here cuts the piece rate when any girl earns over $6.00 per week."

" Cannot the piece rate be cut under Scientific Management? "

Yes, and so can the throat of the goose that laid the golden eggs; but there are a great many incentives put upon the management not to cut the rate once it has been set. For example, for the best results the management must have established the reputation of never having cut a rate which has been set under Scientific Management. Then when a rate has been set and it has been found that no workman or gang boss teacher can teach the actual worker to do the work in the allotted time, the time allowed must be extended. On the other hand, if the time allowed is much longer than that required by the worker to accomplish his task, the management must stand by its mistake and take its medicine; but its medicine will not be bad for it at that. Such "candy work" can be used as a special prize for long service and special compensation for continuous merit.

The rate must not be set until the process and the method for executing the work have been completely changed. When the rate and the task and the method have been determined scientifically and not by rule of thumb, there will be no occasion or desire under Scientific Management to change the rate.   We have seen cases where the earnings of the worker totaled to more than that of the gang bosses and, nevertheless, the unit costs were low.

What are the best remedies for soldiering?

There is but one remedy for soldiering, namely, an accurate knowledge on the part of the management of how much output constitutes a fair day's work, coupled with paying permanently unusually high wages, with no fear of a cut in rate.

CHAPTER III

APPLICATION OF LAWS OF SCIENTIFIC MANAGEMENT

FIELD OF APPLICABILITY

If Scientific Management is so worthy, why are there so few places organized under it at the present time?

Because there are so few engineers and teachers capable of installing it, and they are all busy with more work than they can do. Until some definite method is adopted for increasing the number of teachers, the progress will be slow.

Can Scientific Management be applied to office work, *i.e.* work that is mostly mental work?

Yes, there are many cases where it has been as effective as in the shop or on the job.

On work of repetitive character we have, in several instances, doubled the amount of output per clerk, and shortened the working hours.

We have never seen the case where higher wages, greater output, and lower costs have not resulted when an office force operated under Scientific Management.

What happens when a business is too small or too large to operate under exactly eight functional bosses?

If too small to warrant eight different functional foremen, fewer foremen can be used and each be given a number of functions to perform. If the job is too large for exactly

31

eight men, then there may be several foremen to each function, with an "over foreman" to each group of foremen of the same function. Under the traditional form of management one foreman performs all eight functions as well as the time will permit.

For a description of practical application of Scientific Management, see a series of articles entitled "Applied Methods of Scientific Management," by Frederic A. Parkhurst, running in *Industrial Engineering* for 1911, and published in book form by Wiley & Co.

POSSIBILITY OF SUBSTITUTES FOR SCIENTIFIC MANAGEMENT

Why not get an extra good foreman and simply leave the question of management to him?

In the first place, "extra good foremen" are hard to find, and when found are more profitable to their employer and also themselves when acting in charge of that function for which they are specially fitted.

Furthermore, one man working alone cannot do such efficient work as can several specialists of less brilliancy, in team work, each at the function at which he is specially trained.

As Mr. Ernest Hamlin Abbott has said, in the *Outlook* for Jan. 7, 1911: —

"Scientific Management cannot be 'bought and delivered in a box,' but when it is once installed, it will bring results that cannot be achieved by a merely 'born manager.' If a man wants to practice medicine, it is well if he is a 'born doctor,' but nowadays it is not sufficient; it is not even necessary. So it will be with the manager."

Cannot the American workman devise efficient methods as well as the engineer?

As a proof that the workman cannot compete in devising efficient methods with the trained engineer, it is well to cite the paper 1010 of the Transactions of the American Society of Mechanical Engineers, by Mr. Carl G. Barth, entitled "Slide Rules for the Machine Shop as a part of the Taylor System of Management," in which he states : —

"Thus already during the first three weeks of the application of the slide rules to two lathes, the one a 27 inch, the other a 24 inch, in the larger of these shops, the output of these was increased to such an extent that they quite unexpectedly ran out of work on two different occasions, the consequence being that the superintendent, who had previously worried a good deal about how to get the great amount of work on hand for these lathes out of the way, suddenly found himself confronted with a real difficulty in keeping them supplied with work. But while the truth of this statement may appear quite incredible to a great many persons, to the writer himself, familiar and impressed as he has become with the great intricacy involved in the problem of determining the most economical way of running a machine tool, the application of a rigid mathematical solution to this problem as against the leaving it to the so-called practical judgment and experience of the operator, cannot otherwise result than in the exposure of the perfect folly of the latter method."

What is the reason that employees do not know how fast work should be done?

There are many reasons, such as —

(*a*) They have not investigated their problems by means of motion study and time study.

(b)   They have not realized the importance of having each step in the dependent sequences carried out without delay.

(c)   They have not been taught the saving in time caused by having all of the sequences obvious, and all of the planning and most of the brain work done by the planning department before the work is actually done.

(d)   The workers have been taught, by the fear of running themselves out of a job or having their rate cut, that the safest plan for them is to soldier whenever possible.

(e)   Lack of personal familiarity with stop watch records of elements of work of the best men, under standard conditions, is the cause of their lack of knowledge of how fast the work should be done.

Does not a good system of routing bring nearly all the benefits of Scientific Management?

A system of routing is but a small part of the entire plan of Scientific Management.   It is a very necessary part, however, and the line determining just where routing leaves off and some of the other functions begin is arbitrary.   One man has stated that even motion study is largely a matter of routing the various parts of the human body, particularly the hands, feet, eyes, and head.

For an illuminating discussion of routing and its relation to Scientific Management see "Industrial Plants," by Charles Day, published by *The Engineering Magazine*, 1911.

Is not loyalty and good will the thing that will make employees work most efficiently?

It is certainly a great factor in obtaining coöperation between the management and the workers.   Scientific Management obtains good will by the square deal, by a division of the savings, by teaching, etc., while the old form of management sometimes endeavors to obtain it by jollying, "welfare work," picnics, self-governing committees, etc. The disadvantage of the last is that a self-governing committee does not get the best results, because it is not supplied with and does not know how best to use that data which has been obtained in a scientific manner.

PREPARATION FOR INTRODUCTION OF SCIENTIFIC MANAGEMENT

What preparation can be made for the advent of the Scientific Manager before he comes in?

There are many things that can be done. Among the most necessary and the easiest to do are four : —

(a) Establish standards of methods, and of tools everywhere.

(b) Install schedules and time tables.

(c) Place each man, as far as possible, so that his output and its unit cost shows up separately.

(d) Put present system in writing.

(See "Cost Keeping and Management Engineering," Gillette and Dana.)

These improvements will pay for themselves from the start and will facilitate the work of the efficiency engineer very materially.

PLACE OF INTRODUCTION OF SCIENTIFIC MANAGEMENT

Where is the best place to begin to install Scientific Management?

It should be first installed where it will have the least effect upon the workmen. When changes are to be made that affect the workmen, it is most desirable that those cases should be undertaken first that show most plainly that workmen are benefited and that show up clearest as an object lesson to all the workmen and to all the employers, superintendents, and foremen as to how Scientific Management simultaneously increases wages for the workers and cuts down production costs for the owner. It is desirable to start the installation in many places at the same time. Therefore the establishment of standards everywhere, including standard instruction cards for standard methods, motion study, time study, time cards, records of individual outputs, selecting and training the functional foremen, particularly the foreman in charge of the function of inspection, are the features that should be undertaken at the very first. Collect the great special knowledge that the functional foremen should possess and see that they learn it. In choosing which of two things is to be done first, always give precedence to that which can be nailed down and held from slipping back into the old rut, once it has been made to operate under the new Scientific Management.

METHOD OF INTRODUCTION OF SCIENTIFIC MANAGEMENT

Is it not necessary, in introducing Scientific Management, to import a number of functional foremen, etc.?

That depends upon circumstances. In our business we have a Flying Squadron of "over foremen" for starting a new job properly. These men are trained to handle one or more functions each, and can therefore start the job under Scientific Management on the first day that they arrive. It is their duty to help the permanently assigned functional foremen to get their work into shape and planned ahead as far as possible. The Flying Squadron can then be spared for other work, yet be available in case of emergency. In starting any new undertaking, for best results a larger number of foremen are required than are needed after the job has progressed.

The Flying Squadron, therefore, is valuable at the start of the work for its actual services as well as for teaching the permanent foremen on the job.

How can you introduce Scientific Management into an organization without giving the business a jolt?

By beginning at those places where the savings will be immediate and where changes will affect the entire establishment least, — by installing it first where it affects the work of one man only at a time, and by progressing at that speed that will not cause a jolt to the business.

Time Necessary to Install Scientific Management

How long will it take to install it all?

It can never be "all" installed, because there is no end to it. The time required differs. For example, the Link-Belt Company spent several years putting Scientific Management into their works at Philadelphia, while they were able afterwards to put the same system into their Western shops in less than the same number of months.

It takes much longer to put it in where the management itself must be taught than where there is a Flying Squadron ready to take up the installation of each function.

In construction work, is not the job nearly completed before Scientific Management can be installed?

As there is no end to Scientific Management, it can never be said to be completely installed. In construction work much benefit can be obtained immediately — greater speed, better quality, and lower costs of production. From the very nature of construction work, it is difficult to avoid waste under any plan of management, and particularly under the traditional plan of management. It, therefore, offers unusual opportunities for saving through Scientific Management installed from the first day by the Flying Squadron.

PRACTICABILITY OF SCIENTIFIC MANAGEMENT

Isn't it true that you cannot expect to get all of the men, in fact any man, to use all of the prescribed motions and only the prescribed motions in any one day, or day after day?

It is quite impossible to get perfection in anything. However, the savings in motions, due, for example, to putting the bricks on a packet the right way in the first place, and delivering the brick to the bricklayer exactly in that condition and position that will make it easiest for him to use the most economical motions, together with the gang boss who is specially trained to coach the bricklayer to use the fewest, most economical, and most efficient standard motions, will result in an extremely high efficiency which, even if it does not reach the 100 per cent mark, is nearer to it daily.

How can an engineer tell with a stop watch, by timing a worker for a few hours or days, how much he can do day after day at his work, and how can the engineer be sure that the worker being timed is not using up his reserve strength?

He cannot be sure without sufficiently painstaking investigation. That is why Dr. Taylor timed men for long periods before he found his laws relating to quantities of rest required for overcoming fatigue without calling upon the worker's reserve strength. No worker has ever considered that he must actually rest two whole hours in a day, yet Dr. Taylor found that some kinds of work required the worker to rest over 50 per cent of his entire day.

Purpose of Scientific Management

Is it not true that under the Taylor System the shop or the business " exists first, last, and all the time for the purpose of paying dividends to its owners "?

Yes, and that is also true about shops and businesses under any and all other forms of management. Without dividends there is no doubt that the best thing to do would be to sell off the machinery before it was all worn out, and to do such other things as might be necessary to get back the capital invested before it was lost.

Expense

Must one " go the whole game " with Scientific Management to get real results?

No. Especially is this true in the small concern where there are not enough employees to warrant the installa-

tion of all of the features of Scientific Management.
A small concern can use many of the features, however,
very advantageously.

**Can saving be made, and have savings been made,
from the first day?**

Savings by use of Scientific Management can undoubtedly be made from the first day.   Scientific investigations can undoubtedly be made that will pay for themselves as they go along; but the relation of the saving by
Scientific Management to the expense of it varies at
different periods, and depends upon how fast Scientific
Management is installed and upon the nature of the
business.

In our business, we can show hundreds of instances
on the cost records of substantial decrease in costs, in
many cases of costs that were halved as fast as the system
was installed.

**Is it not necessary to wait years after Scientific Man-
agement is introduced to get full reduction in costs?**

Yes, in a business already highly systematized, it undoubtedly will require from 2 to 4 years to get the full
benefit of the complete introduction of Scientific Management.   This time can usually be reduced when there is
no interference from those who oppose through ignorance.

**Does not Scientific Management occasion a large out-
lay for equipment and machinery?**

The purpose of Scientific Management is not the installing of the best machinery, although the best machin-

ery is of course desirable. It is using to best advantage the machinery available.

Scientific Management aims, primarily, so to handle labor with the existing machinery that the maximum prosperity will result for the employer and for all employees. But, as it deals largely with scientific investigation, it discovers laws, and points out the economic advantages of new devices and machines. While it makes the employee more efficient and the management of more assistance to the employees, it also predetermines and makes inventions in machinery as well as methods almost obvious. Whether or not additional machinery and equipment is acquired is not a vital part of Scientific Management.

Is not the expense burden of maintaining the planning department equal to all the savings that it can make?

Dr. Taylor answers this in a most concise manner in paragraph 155 in the Transactions of the American Society of Mechanical Engineers, Paper 1003 ("Shop Management," Harper and Brothers, pp. 55–56) : —

"At first view the running of a planning department, together with the other innovations, would appear to involve a large amount of additional work and expense, and the most natural question would be whether the increased efficiency of the shop more than offsets this outlay.

"It must be borne in mind, however, that, with the exception of the study of unit times, there is hardly a single item of work done in the planning department which is not already being done in the shop. Establishing a planning department merely concentrates the planning and much other brain work in a few men especially fitted for their task and trained in their especial lines, instead of having it done, as heretofore, in most cases by high-priced mechanics, well fitted to work at their trades, but poorly trained for work more or less clerical in its nature."

Mr. H. L. Gantt says, page 18, in "Work, Wages, and Profits": —

"A scientific investigation into the details of a condition that has grown up unassisted by science has never yet failed to show that economies and improvements are feasible that benefit both parties to an extent unexpected by either."

Is not Scientific Time Study so expensive that the average job cannot afford it?

Scientific Time Study does not all have to be done on one job. There are certain features that will reduce costs from the first day that can be done on even small jobs. The average job, even the small job, can be helped by many of the features of Scientific Management; and the instruction cards of previous jobs can be used with great economy even on small jobs.

Why are so many more inspectors required if the work is done better under Scientific Management?

Because the instruction cards call for a definite quality. They do not call for having the "work done to the satisfaction" of anybody. The extra money paid to the workers under Scientific Management is contingent upon the prescribed kind of quality being achieved.

The inspector keeps a close watch of work under Scientific Management. It is his duty to detect mistakes or lack of quality before much damage is done. As an example, suppose a workman was ordered to make 100 duplicate pieces from the same drawing. The inspector would watch the first piece keenly during its making and would pass upon the first unit when it was finished, to make sure that the workman understood his duties, and what was expected of him, and also that the quality of the work was right in every particular.

To catch mistakes before they are made is the cheapest way to get the right results.

Furthermore, the inspector under Scientific Management not only inspects, but also assists and instructs the workmen directly instead of through the other functional foremen.

Isn't there a larger waste from spoiling materials under Scientific Management?

There is not, because, as stated elsewhere, the first functional foreman introduced is that of inspector. The work is inspected more systematically under Scientific Management. The bonus is not paid unless the quality is within the requirements of the written instruction card.

The method of inspection under traditional management is often wasteful, because the inspection is usually done after the material is fabricated. Under Scientific Management the inspection proceeds as does the work itself. Inasmuch as the gang boss gets no bonus if the quality is not in accordance with the prescribed quality, he has a constant incentive to play at team work with the workman, *i.e.* he sees that the workman is provided with tools and surroundings in the best condition to make the prescribed quality. It is a matter of history that the quality of output has invariably improved by the introduction of Scientific Management.

INDICATORS OF SUCCESSFUL MANAGEMENT

What indicates the quality of the Management?

The best indicator of the quality of the management is the difference between the *customary* wages given for a certain kind of work and also the usual costs of production for that kind of work in other establishments, compared with the wages given and the costs of production in the works under consideration; or, in other words, the amount that the wages are higher and the amount that the costs of production are lower than usual, indicate the quality of management — other qualities, such as sanitary conditions, being as good or better.

If Scientific Management is all that is claimed for it, why are not the dividends always larger than in any shop where there is no Scientific Management?

They would be, if the merit and quality of the management were the one determining factor in profits and dividends. On the contrary, business judgment as to what and when to buy and where to sell, good salesmanship, and ability to get business at high prices are often of such great importance that dividends can be paid in spite of bad management. On the other hand, there are some cases where the management is so good that dividends can be paid in spite of bad business handling.

CHAPTER IV

EFFECT OF SCIENTIFIC MANAGEMENT ON THE WORKER

ACCIDENTS

Does Scientific Management insure the workman against accidents?

It does not insure him, but it certainly does reduce the number of accidents, because the machines, scaffolds, works, and ways are made and maintained in the standard condition called for on the instruction card, and are regularly inspected and overhauled as directed, and as often as required, by the written orders that come regularly from the Tickler or Reminder File.

Does not intensive production cause rapid depreciation of machinery, causing bad work and accidents and injury to the men?

No, because the desired maintainable standard condition of the machinery is determined by the planning department, just the same as the speed at which it is to be operated. It is inspected, cleaned and oiled, and repaired at stated times, whether it needs it or not. It must be kept up to the standard condition, or the worker cannot get the big outputs called for in order to get his bonus.

Therefore, the machinery is maintained constantly in such a condition that it will not break down or cause accidents. In fact, this function of repairs and maintenance at prescribed condition is assigned to a functional foreman specially trained to look after this work in accordance with the written instructions furnished by the planning department.

Does not a bonus scheme cause the work to be slighted and result in accidents to those who work under such conditions?

Yes, it does, when the bonus scheme is applied under the old plans of management. One man has stated that "any bonus scheme for repairing locomotives should be prohibited by laws; because when so many lives are dependent upon the quality of repairs on a locomotive, there should never be an incentive to hurry the mechanic doing the repairs."

Under all of the old forms of "bonus schemes" this is absolutely true. Dr. Taylor must have recognized this and all other perfectly obvious difficulties of management in his practice. Dr. Taylor also successfully provided for overcoming this difficulty in a most logical and efficient manner, as follows:—

First, he analyzed the problem.
Second, he broke it up into its several most elementary subdivisions.
Third, he applied science to solving the problem of handling each subdivision in the best way.
Fourth, he built up, by and with the advice and assistance of the best workmen and engineers obtainable, a complete new process synthetically.
Fifth, he caused to be put in writing the entire process, so that it could be used forevermore, with all the ad-

vantages that come from conserving the information of how to do a thing in the best known way.

Sixth, he created the function of inspector, with duties of constructive criticism and not destructive criticism. He made it the duty of the inspector to sign a separate paper, stating that each and every repair had been executed precisely in accordance with the demanded quality of workmanship — no better and no worse. He authorized the inspector to deal directly with the workman and to assist him to achieve the prescribed quality of workmanship.

Seventh, he required the foreman to sign a separate piece of paper stating the length of time required to complete the job in the prescribed manner according to the requirements of the instruction card, as certified to in writing by the inspector.

Eighth, he provided that if the workman did the job exactly as prescribed, and certified to by the inspector, and if he also did the job within a certain time, he got a bonus — otherwise he did not.

It is now obvious that on such important matters as repairs on locomotives the Taylor plan is the most efficient for prevention of accidents. In our own experience, we have found that Dr. Taylor's plan is of great assistance in preventing accidents; in fact, we know that it is the one simplest and most efficient method of protecting the workers from injury and loss of life.

Dr. Taylor's plan is usually discussed from the standpoint of reducing costs, raising wages, increasing speed of construction, etc.; but if it had no other merit than its great benefits in eliminating the horrors and wastes due to the injury and killing of human beings, both of the public and of the workers themselves, it would have warranted the life work of Dr. Taylor and his followers spent in the creation of the science.

Brain

How can you expect every laborer to understand Scientific Management when it takes an engineer so many years to learn it?

The laborer does not understand it, nor is he expected to understand it. He simply understands the assistance he receives from the functional foremen in learning how to do his work more efficiently. He recognizes that he gets fairer treatment from the disciplinarian, higher wages from the time and cost clerk, and much more help from all the functional foremen; but he does not always learn the theories of Scientific Management unless he is ambitious enough specially to study it and to follow the same road that is open to every one else.

A machinist who has worked under Scientific Management for about one half of the ten years of his experience was asked how he liked the system. His reply was that he didn't know much about the system, because he "personally did not come in contact with it." He further stated that about all he knew of it was that somehow it enabled him to earn about a third more money every week of his life and that he had never been treated as well in any other establishment.

How long will it take any man to learn it?

There will never be a time when the expert will not learn more about it. The more one studies Scientific Management the more one is able to see what there is to learn, and the more experience he has in it the faster he is able to acquire new facts about it.

At the present time it is considered that a liberal education, preferably in engineering, followed by the complete mastery of at least one and preferably several mechanical trades, followed by four to six years of the closest study of the practical applications of the laws of Scientific Management in several widely different kinds of work, should make one capable of installing nearly all portions of Scientific Management into any business. In other words, with the same quality of brains, application, study, and experience, about the same length of time is required as to become a skilled surgeon. The surgeon, however, has the advantage of having at his disposal a tremendous amount of literature on his subject and also educational institutions. These, though quite as desirable, are not in existence in the subject of management. It is to be hoped, however, that this condition will be altered in the future and the time necessary for preparation will be greatly reduced.

Does it not make machines out of men?

Now, this question is usually asked in just this form, but there seems to be a great difference of opinion as to exactly what the questioner means. Is a good boxer, or fencer, or golf player a machine? Is the highly trained soldier at bayonet or saber drill a machine? He certainly approaches closely the 100 per cent mark of perfection from the standpoint of the experts in motion study. It is not nearly so important to decide whether or not he is a machine as to decide whether or not it is desirable to have a man trained as near perfection as possible in accordance with that method that expert investigators, working in harmony with the best actual workers, have decided to be the best known method for executing a given piece of work.

"All-around experience" to-day often means undue familiarity with many wrong methods, and "judgment" too often means the sad memory of the details of having done the work in several inefficient ways with a memory good enough to prevent repeating the use of the worst methods.

It is the aim of Scientific Management to induce men to act as nearly like machines as possible, so far as doing the work in the one best way that has been discovered is concerned. After the worker has learned that best way, he will have a starting point from which to measure any new method that his ingenuity can suggest. But until he has studied and mastered the standard method, he is requested not to start a debating society on that subject. Experience has shown that, with the best men chosen for the special work of selecting the method and planning the various steps in the processes, — these men having facilities and data at their command that equip them for their jobs, — their way will, in most cases, be better than that of the worker who has not first qualified on their way.

Experience has also shown that, whether or not the men may be called machines, they fare better and profit more when the management takes the time to have a trained planning department, coöperating with the best workmen, determining every step in the process, and every motion in the step, and the effect of every variable in the motion. Then, after the "machine" has done it that way, — in the time allowed for the way, — the "machine" will be paid unusually high wages in real money for any suggestions that will be more efficient. He will be promoted to teach the others his new accepted method. If he continues to make suggestions for better methods than those of the planning department, he will be promoted to it. The line of promotion continues still higher; in fact, this "machine" will find himself at the top, if the measuring methods and devices show him to be more efficient than his fellows, for Scientific Management boosts "machines" for efficiency, not for their bluffs, bulldozing, or snap judgment.

Doesn't Scientific Management keep the worker from being an all-around mechanic and instead make him a narrowly trained specialist?

Perhaps so. Is it not better so? When there is so much to learn about such a simple thing as transporting a brick from the street to its final resting place, it is not better for the worker to have 100 per cent of knowledge on one specialty than to have one half per cent of his total knowledge on each of 200 different ways of earning a living. In all the great professions, specialization is the order of the day.

The physician and surgeon is no longer also the dentist. The dentist no longer attempts to do everything in his profession, except in remote places. He specializes in one of the many subdivisions of dentistry. His mechanical laboratory work certainly requires a differently trained expert than does the specialty of orthodontia or prophy-laxis

There is so much to learn in any kind of work that the most highly specialized worker can never expect to learn it all.   In the professions, specialization generally means increased standing, usefulness, and earning power.   Experience has proved that this is also true in the arts and trades.

Dr. Taylor has spent years investigating the comparatively simple art of shoveling, and he has said that even yet he has not learned it all.   In case any one feels cramped by narrow overspecialization, he has as further compensation the fact that, if he has learned it all, his brain will be in such rested condition at the close of the working day that he can attend some night manual training school, where motion study, time study, and standardization are *not* taught, and where the faculty prove nightly that the Taylor plan of management, as a practical proposition, is not worthy of his consideration, because if it were they would, of course, teach it.

Perhaps specialization does narrow the mechanic, from the viewpoint of some people, but it does make him a highly trained expert in his specialty.

In case he loses his job under Scientific Management, is he not too highly specialized and not enough of an all-around mechanic to hold a job anywhere else?

The answer is "No."   For he has been taught a method of attack that will enable him to use to advantage all the brains he has.   He will have been taught all economies from motion study.   That, in itself, will enable him to excel quickly those workers who have not been so taught. He will have been taught the economies resulting from the use of the instruction card.

If he has been taught to a point where he has been "overspecialized," then he surely has been taught habits of work that will enable him to become quickly a profitable worker at any new work that he may undertake.

Does not the monotony of the highly specialized subdivision of work cause the men to become insane?

No. Until one has worked under Scientific Management, and consequently realizes what the subdivisions mean, one cannot realize the great amount of knowledge that it is possible to acquire on any one subdivision of any one trade. For example, it was not until after we devoted years to the study of the motions used by several mechanical trades that we discovered that with the aid of a few devices we could teach an apprentice to lay brick faster and make a better looking and stronger wall than could an experienced journeyman working in the old manner.

Further study shows that our more recent investigations cause the old methods of bricklaying to be obsolete, for we now can build brick walls by machinery, at a lower cost, with no question as to filling of the joints, stronger, quicker, and drier, and by the same methods can build any kind of arches, ornamental work, etc., as cheaply as straight and plain brickwork can be built under the old method. We now see possibilities of improvement under this new method that seem to have no end. Yet, generally speaking, is not the subdivision of the mason's trade, brickwork, considered as monotonous as any kind of work?

A few years ago it was a general custom all over America, and is still in remote places, for a "mason" to be a stone mason, stone cutter, bricklayer, plasterer, and cement worker. Modern conditions have reclassified these trades, so that even the subclasses of the bricklayers now are divided into several distinct classes. The best plasterers and stone masons can no longer compete with the best bricklayer on brickwork. The plasterer's trade is also subdivided, although not as much as it will be.

To the man who has no leaning toward brain work, there is an ideal place provided in the performing department. When he feels that his work there is monotonous, there are three opportunities open to him —

(a) He may join the planning department.

(b) He may become teacher of the other men who prefer the so-called monotonous work, relieved of all responsibility except to do their work as called for.

(c) He can plan the spending of the extra money that will be in his pay envelope on next pay day, and can consider the intellectual stimulus that the extra pay will purchase; for when work is so highly repetitive as to be monotonous, it will surely enable the man best fitted for that work to earn the highest wages that he can ever earn at any vocation, *because* he has had practice at that work so long that it has become monotonous.

No, he will not become insane, for if his brain is of such an order that his work does not stimulate it to its highest degree, then he will be promoted, for under Scientific Management each man is specially trained to occupy that place that is the highest that he is capable, mentally and physically, of filling, after having had long training by the best teachers procurable.

Does it not rest a man to use different motions and doesn't it refresh his brain to do the work in a different way each time?

As a general proposition, it does *not* refresh a worker to use different motions. When it does, the planning should and does take that into consideration when making out the instruction card. One of the most generally recognized instances of this is the bookkeeper's standing desk and high chair. He changes from sitting to standing and *vice versa*, to rest and refresh himself; yet the motions of work are identical whether standing or sitting. That doing work the same way requires less effort than doing it it a new way is so well recognized that a condition finally results where it seems as if the fingers could do the work with no other assistance than the command from the brain to proceed. This condition is called being "fingerwise" at a piece of work. It is well illustrated by the simple process of "buttoning a button," an act most complicated to the beginner.

Different motions each time require additional effort, a new mental process and a complete decision with the accompanying extra fatigue. The same motions each time take advantage of automaticity of motions, which is often less fatiguing than less wasteful, though constantly differing, motions.

Does not the old-fashioned way of gaining experience or judgment give the worker a training that he would never get otherwise?

Yes. The methods of Scientific Management will deprive him of much of the unnecessary and unproductive part of his experience, in that it will teach him, in the quickest way, how to learn the most efficient method. If he gets such proper training first, it will provide him during his after life with a mental and manual equipment that will serve him in making quick decisions in selecting his future experience, and in judging the "old type of experience" wherever he encounters it later.

"Experience is the best teacher" is as meaningless a proverb as "You can't teach an old dog new tricks." When the best experience has been found, measured, and recognized, it should be made standard, — written down on an instruction card. In this form it can be depended upon to be the best teacher, for it will transmit the information and experience from one mechanic to another without any loss in transmission.

Chance for a Square Deal

How can any one think it fair to take stop watch records on the very best man obtainable and then expect the others of the rank and file to keep up with such records?

Scientific Management does not expect the inefficient man to keep up with the first-class man, neither does it expect a dollar watch to do the work of the $300 watch. But when standards are created they must be founded on the work of the best man procurable, *i.e.* they must be a "100 per cent standard man's" records. Then all due allowance must be made for the difference in quality between the record of the standard worker and the worker who is actually going to do the work.

The poorer quality of men are not able to equal the records of the best men, but the analysis of data will show at what speed each man should work for the best combined results of output and health. Obviously it would add too much to fixed charges to take time study on each man. The present method is, by comparison, cheaper and more just, fair, effective, and satisfactory.

What show of a square deal has a worker who has from " one to eight foremen standing over him at the same time, applying a sort of industrial Third Degree " to make him conform to the desired standard motions?

This question has nothing to do with Taylor's plan of management, for the reason that each foreman helps the worker to do his work in the prescribed manner; teaches him the standard method, and how to use the least fatiguing and non-wasteful motions. Regardless of the number that may be helping him at once, the gang bosses have nothing to do with any "third degree" nor with any other form of discipline. That is all taken care of by an unprejudiced specialist called the "disciplinarian," whose make-up is that of peacemaker and whose duty is the furthering of the square deal.

CHANCE FOR WORK

When Scientific Management is in full operation, can the management dispense with the good men?

On the contrary, under Scientific Management even the functional foremen are expected to acquire so much more knowledge about their one function than is customary under the traditional plan of management that it will always require particularly good men to fill their positions.

The men, in their turn, that will be required, on account of the large outputs and the close following of the instruction cards demanded, will have to be exceptionally good men of their class. Every man will be expected to be the best obtainable of his respective class. In fact, Scientific Management goes farthest into the subject of selecting men specially fitted for their work. It does, however, demand that a man shall have a great deal of knowledge about his specialty and life work, rather than a little knowledge about many kinds of work.

Not only does Scientific Management require good men after it is in full operation, but it also provides for definite promotion to retain a man after he has outgrown his job. As Mr. James F. Butterworth, a well-known English authority, summed it up in the *London Standard* — "Scientific Management not only quickly recognizes the first-class man, but attracts other first-class men to share in the bettered conditions."

Granted that Scientific Management is advantageous for the best worker, is it not a distinct hardship to the mediocre man?

It is not, because first of all, the best men are promoted out of competition with the mediocre man. Furthermore, every man, including the mediocre man, is taught and promoted to fill the highest place that he is by nature and special training able to occupy. In fact, every man is taught and coached and helped until he reaches an earning power that he never could expect under the traditional form of management. The average man, having been taught a systematic method of attack, is better prepared to handle any new work at which he is put than he ever could if he had not had the experience under the systematic working of Scientific Management.

Does not Scientific Management eliminate many men, *i.e.* actually reduce the number of men employed, according to Mr. Taylor's own words?

No, because the management is enabled to handle more men and thus get the work completed quicker. Furthermore, while it is true that on any one part of the work the men required might be fewer, it is also true that the method of selection itself often results in providing the men, who are eliminated because of natural unfitness, with work for which they in turn are much better fitted. Actual statistics show that there has never been a case where the total number of employees has remained less in any organization operating under Scientific Management.

What would happen if every concern suddenly were able to do its work with one third of its present number of men?

It will take two or three years to install the principal features of Scientific Management in any one concern. It would take a lifetime to install all of the refinements of Scientific Management now recognized and determined. There never has been a case yet where the business being systematized did not employ a total of more men the more highly it was systematized. As soon as the work in any one department can be done with fewer men, the business as a whole becomes so successful that it can underbid its competitors; in fact, it often creates a market for its goods and then requires more men in other departments.

What becomes of the men to-day under the traditional plan of management?

Under this old plan, often the efficient instead of the inefficient man is "weeded out." He is never sure of his job, because usually under the old plan there is no accurate measuring of his efficiency. Where there is, he very often has made a low record of output because of a fault of the management.

Perhaps in some "dependent sequence," his work has been held up by failure of the management to supply him something; for example, the carpenter cannot lay the floor if he is not supplied with nails. The shoveler's output might be low because he had not been furnished with shovels that would permit of $21\frac{1}{2}$ pounds of material on the shovel regardless of the change in the kind of materials shoveled.

"By those who have grasped this fact it is universally held that increased production due to efficiency of labor accrues very largely to the laborers themselves." ("Economics," by Arthur Twining Hadley.)

What happens to unskilled labor under Scientific Management?

Under Scientific Management there is no unskilled labor; or, at least, labor does not remain unskilled. Unskilled labor is taught the best method obtainable, and is provided with a corps of teachers whose duty it is to assist the laborers to become highly skilled in that art or trade at which they work.

Furthermore, the men are promoted as fast as they are fitted to be promoted, and are specially taught to fill places commanding higher wages even while they are taught. No labor is unskilled after it is taught.

Will not Scientific Management result in putting unskilled laborers at mechanics' work?

Not while they are unskilled. It is a part of the system to train all men to perform the highest class of work which they are mentally and physically able to perform. It in no way, however, contemplates the superseding of mechanics; which, of course, would be bad for the mechanics. The mechanics need have no fear from that source; in fact, Scientific Management plans for and entails so high a degree of perfection that the one greatest difficulty it encounters is to secure mechanics of sufficient intelligence, training, and expertness to carry out its plan. It does not concur, however, with the once general belief and principle that a locomotive driver should also be an expert machinist who could build as well as run a locomotive.

Is it not specially hard on the " weaker brothers "?

Yes, if "weaker brothers" means unwilling incompetents. These, Scientific Management discards, as does every other form of management, as fast as they can be detected. Any body of workers who, by purposely hiding the "weaker brother" in the gang, thereby make it difficult and sometimes impossible for the old-fashioned management to detect the weaker brother, is paying for his support out of the pockets of the strong. If this is so, why not measure his ability, pay him accurately what he is worth, pay the strong ones accordingly, and let the strong pay him what extra amount they desire to contribute on account of his weakness? Meanwhile, perhaps, he could be taught, or put on work where he would be more efficient.

Oftentimes a worker is inefficient because he is naturally unfitted for his chosen work by reason of natural slowness of successive action or poor ability for retention in memory of spoken words. Those workers with high personal coefficient, where the inward end organ most used in the work is the eye, as in the work of proofreading, are often the fastest workers when changed to such work, for example, as short-hand, where the impressions on the brain are taken in at the ear.

Again, the measuring devices of Scientific Management often discover that the "weaker brother," or the inefficient sister, is really a square peg in a round hole. While all kinds of management endeavor to discard the inferior workers, Scientific Management is the one plan that makes definite and systematic effort to promote each worker to the highest notch he is capable of in his chosen life work. It tries to place each worker where scientific investigation and analysis of his individual peculiarities indicate that he will be most efficient.

Volumes could be written about the worker who is in the wrong life work, for which he is by nature totally unfitted. The recognition of this fact is the cause for the interest in vocational guidance throughout the country.

We believe that one great benefit derived from Scientific

Management will be the utilization of its data for assisting young men and women in determining the life work for which their particular faculties will enable them to be most efficient. Scientific Management endeavors to discover for workers, before they go to work, that work to which they are best adapted. In fact, the selection of the worker is an act of great importance under Scientific Management, and is one on which great stress is laid.

Scientific Management also tries to discard no man who has been tried out and partially taught. It attempts to place him to better advantage to himself and also to the management.

What happens to the inefficient worker? Is he not thrown out upon the labor market?

There are several things that may happen to him.

(*a*) He may be taught so that he becomes extremely efficient.

(*b*) His efficiency will be increased, whatever it is.

(*c*) He may be placed at a kind of work for which he is better fitted.

(*d*) He may be placed on that portion of the work that has not been systematized. There has never been a case where the Taylor System caused a large number of unemployed.

Doesn't the Taylor System really plan to eliminate the hopelessly inefficient man?

Yes, and so does every other plan of management. The other plans are not fair in that they do not always determine which are the really inefficient, but leave it to an overworked, busy, uninformed, prejudiced foreman or employer; while under the Taylor System the man is taught, shifted, and taught again, until he is placed at that work at which he is most efficient, and tried and tried until he has demonstrated his entire unfitness. Meantime, while he may not have been able to earn the maximum wages, he will have earned much higher wages than he could earn anywhere else on similar work under the old form of management.

HEALTH

What regard has this System for the physical welfare of the men? Does not this System call upon the reserve force of the worker, and thus wear him out before his time?

This question is answered at length by Mr. C. A. E. Winslow, Associate Professor of Biology, College of the City of New York, and Curator of Public Health, American Museum of Natural History, New York, in an intensely interesting paper read before the Congress of Technology on the fiftieth anniversary of the granting of the charter of the Massachusetts Institute of Technology. Professor Winslow states in the closing paragraph: —

"The cleanliness of the factory, the purity of the drinking water, the quality of lighting, the sanitary provisions, and a dozen other points will suggest themselves to the skilled investigator when on the ground. He may find in many of these directions economic methods by which efficiency may be promoted."

Have observations ever been made on any one man long enough to determine if Scientific Management benefits him?

Yes, and on hundreds of men. A visit to the Tabor Manufacturing Co., the Link-Belt Co., and the J. M.

Dodge Co. will convince any one who looks the employees over. There one finds that the men are happier, healthier, better paid, and in better condition every way than the men found in similar work in that vicinity. These places above named are among the shops where Scientific Management in its highest form has been in operation the longest time.

Does not the "speed boss" speed up the men to a point that is injurious to their health?

"Speed boss," like "task," is an unfortunate name, but, as Mr. James M. Dodge has said, the word "task" will probably have to be used until a word that is more descriptive can be substituted for it.

The same thing is true of "speed boss." We have heard one orator state that "the speed boss is the man who drives the slaves." He is right if you call the *machines* the slaves, for the "speed boss" does not tell the men how fast they shall make their motions. He does, however, tell the men at what speeds their machines shall run. He does not drive the men at all. He is their servant. When they cannot make the machines work at the speed called for on the instruction card, it is up to him to do it, then to teach them, or else to report to the planning department that he cannot, and then its members must show and help him. Under the traditional plan of management, swearing at a man is supposed to make him work faster, for the time being at least. The speed boss's job is to swear at the machine if he wants to, but he must attain the speed called for, no faster and no slower, or he does not earn his bonus.

Under the old form of management it sometimes happens that the foreman gets so angry at the machine that he discharges the operator, but the speed boss can not do this under Scientific Management.   All cases of discharge must be handled by a trained, quiet disciplinarian, who disciplines the operator, the speed boss, and any one else who needs it, even the superintendent himself.   This, in itself, is so unusual that in many cases the average workman cannot understand how it is that he is being treated so fairly.

As a general practice, do the people want a standard of efficiency so high that it requires a stop watch to get "the last drop of blood"?

There is no "last drop of blood" about it!   The stop watch is a measuring device that has no more to do with making men work than it has when used by a physician to determine at what rate the pulse is beating.   The stop watch is used to determine the correct time necessary for doing a certain piece of work, and to determine how much the worker should rest in order to achieve and maintain his best physical and mental condition.

It must be admitted, even by those who do not understand Scientific Management, that there is some rate of speed which is the correct speed at which the individual worker should work, and that this speed varies according to the man — his birth, education, training, health, and condition.

This correct speed is not the speed at which he would like to work if he were just naturally lazy, but it is the best speed at which he can work day after day, month after month, and, if he has reached the zenith of his promotion, then also year after year, and thrive, and continually improve in health.

The stop watch must be used to insure that the instruction card, the output, the percentage of rest for overcoming fatigue, and the pay shall be based upon that exact speed.

Taylor has found, by use of the stop watch and by timing thousands of cases, that some work requires that a man shall actually rest over 50 per cent of the entire day, and that practically all work requires more than $12\frac{1}{2}$ per cent rest. Now, that is one hour in an eight-hour day, and it does not sound nearly as much like "taking the last drop of blood" as does the old method of management, under which, if the manager heard that the man rested one half hour every day, he saw to it that the man was discharged.

Wherein does it cost the employer anything to lose a worker by wearing him out?

It takes time and costs money to specially train him, and old workers are therefore usually the most desirable.

INITIATIVE

What has Scientific Management to take the place of the ingenious man?

It has nothing "to take the place of the ingenious man." It does not supplant him. On the contrary, it furnishes a specially equipped planning department to help him to further and conserve systematically his ingenuity.

This department works out problems of improvement of methods and conditions.

Such a department puts the services of the ingenious man and the inventor on a business basis and provides measuring devices and methods for determining the numerical measure of the efficiency of the new methods as compared with the old.

Does not the management lose the initiative and the bright ideas of its ingenious employees when they are obliged to follow implicitly the detailed written orders of the instruction card?

No. On the contrary, there is a special department for the employment of those men whose make-up and training specially fit them to make the most numerous and most valuable suggestions for improvements.

The value of the ingenious suggestions of the workmen is specially recognized and provided for by Scientific Management. Not only is a department created and maintained for fostering, conserving, and specially inventing such forms of improvement, but also a cash prize system is in operation for further obtaining the suggestions of those workmen who are outside the regular planning department.

It is seldom appreciated by the layman that the only inventions and improvements that are not wanted are those that are offered by the employee *before* he has first qualified on the standard method of procedure in accordance with the much tried out instruction card.

The condition precedent to an audience for offering a suggestion for an improvement is to have proved that the suggestor knows the standard method, and can do the work in the standard way of standard quality in the standard time. Having thus qualified, he is in a position to know whether or not his new suggestion is a real improvement.

Scientific Management offers the first standard method of obtaining high efficiency from those best qualified to invent and to make new methods. The ingenious employee is specially protected, assisted, and encouraged.

Does not standardization dwarf, wither, and preclude innovation and improvement?

On the contrary, standardization offers a base line from which we can measure efficiency. Inasmuch as the value of the entire scheme of scientific management hangs on time study, much time study must, therefore, be taken and used. This consumes time and costs much money. The fewer the standards the less quantity of time study need be taken.

Therefore, for the best net results, a few well-chosen, first-class standards are much to be preferred to many ill-chosen imperfect standards.

Standardization enables, and offers a constant incentive to, employees to try for better standards, not only for the joy of achieving, but also for the money reward that comes from making a better standard. The history of Scientific Management shows greater improvement under it than under any other plan.

When a man is paid under the day work plan for his time instead of for the quantity of output of prescribed quality, there is little to cause him to devise new methods or ways to increase his efficiency or productivity.

On the other hand, under Scientific Management he being paid for his productivity, there is every incentive to do all that he can, — to invent new ways, less wasteful ways, and to keep himself in the best physical condition to work.

What is there in it for the workman who makes the suggestion?

There are various rewards for accepted suggestions: sometimes cash; sometimes promotion to teacher or gang boss; sometimes the saving that the suggestion makes for a definite period of time; or a combination of the above accompanied by the recognition of having the accepted new tool or method named after the suggestor.

INSTRUCTION

Do not men dislike to be taught by teachers from outside?

Sometimes they do dislike it at first, but they usually like obtaining additional information about their life work, regardless from what source it comes.

Furthermore, the teaching usually comes mostly from the men who have been selected from their own number. The extra money that the teachers get is an added incentive to them to learn, earn more while learning, and thus be better fitted for promotion to the position of teacher.

Don't the workers think they " know it all " to start with?

Many mechanics believe that the best workmen of their trade do know nearly all that is worth knowing about their trade, but the unit cost columns and other devices for measuring efficiency soon shows them that "the way we have always done it" can usually be improved upon.

Do the men really benefit much by the teaching, or does not the benefit all go to the employer?

In re teaching, Mr. William Dana Orcutt says:—

"The ambitious workman of the past has sought to advance himself by attending night school, and in other ways which are a strain upon the time which he requires for rest and recreation. Scientific Management gives him this opportunity, under the most skillful instructors, while actually employed in his day's labors, fitting him, at the expense of the concern which employs him, to become qualified to earn higher wages from the very source which gives him his education."

What incentive has the teacher to see that the workers are properly trained?

The teacher's promotion depends on his success in getting results from the workers under his instruction.

He also gets a bonus every time that a worker gets a bonus and a second or double bonus every time that every worker in his entire gang gets a bonus.

Does not Scientific Management do away with the old "journeyman" idea, and is not that of itself a distinct disadvantage to the men?

It does sometimes do away with the "old journeyman idea" in many ways, especially with several of its wasteful aspects. It does away with teaching the apprentice by word of mouth by the traditionally taught journeyman, who has no idea of pedagogy. It does away with taking advantage of an apprentice for a certain definite number of years, just because he is an apprentice. It pays the apprentice in accordance with the quality and quantity of his output, instead of paying him a boy's wages even when he does a man's quantity of work.

It does away with the infamous and common practice of limiting the age at which an apprentice may start to learn his trade. It recognizes no such rule as that a boy shall not begin to lay brick after he is eighteen and shall not be out of his time before he is twenty-one, regardless of how expert he may be. It accords no special favors to any boy because his father was of the trade at which the boy works.

It substitutes for all this a square deal and a more efficient method of teaching the trade to a boy. It enables him to learn faster, to learn the science of his trade, to learn the best method that science can devise. It furnishes specially taught teachers to give "post-journeyman instruction" to even its best men. It makes available for use as a wage-earning device all of the expert knowledge that constant investigation, analysis, and study can devise, collect, and conserve.

Does not the paying of the bonus to the foreman make him help the best workers and let the poorer workers shift for themselves?

He must also help the poor workers or he does not get his second bonus, as the task set is achievable by any persistent worker. As the records of the foremen's gangs are watched by the superintendent, any foreman who

does not teach all of his men so that they all can attain
their task would not last long at his job.

LEISURE OR REST

**Granted that workers "soldier," what is the
harm? Does not that rest them?**

A certain percentage of rest is necessary for the workers.
It is absolutely required for their health. Under Scientific Management the amount of rest is determined scientifically; it is not guessed. The men are required to
rest. On our own work we have demonstrated that
regular enforced rest periods have invariably resulted
in reduced costs of production. Soldiering is a case of
making believe that outputs are produced when they
are not. It is the worst form of cheating that there is.
It often makes men work as hard in pretending to work
as they would in actually producing output. Soldiering
results in lower wages to the workers and in a business
decline to the community.

LIFE, LIBERTY, AND THE PURSUIT OF HAPPINESS

**Does not Scientific Management interfere with the
workman's personal liberty?**

If by that is meant the privilege of doing the work any
way he chooses, or by any method, or on a standard of
quality other than that prescribed, the answer is certainly "yes." But in every other respect, "no." His
freedom from petty graft and holdup, and the protec-
tion and square deal offered him, give him more net liberty than he receives under any other plan of management.

**Does not the forcing of the workmen to use the speci-
fied motions of the System only, from the time they arrive
in the morning until they leave at night, take away their
liberty and enforce slavery conditions upon the workers?**

It has never been contemplated to prescribe each and
every motion from the time of arrival to the time of
departure in a mill or on a job any more than on a
golf course or a baseball field. It is, however, hoped
and expected that those motions that are of no use
will be eliminated as far as possible, and that the
motions used will be limited as far as possible to those
that produce output or cause restful exercise. Surely
no thinking man wants the work so arranged that
the worker makes useless motions, — useless either to
himself or to his employer.

Go to any library or sporting goods store, and you can
obtain many books with copious illustrations reproduced
from photographs to illustrate how to make the exact
motions for the greatest efficiency in many different kinds
of sports. But in how many trades can similar books
be found? The best example to date of applying the
motion studies of the arts of war to the arts of peace can
be seen in Dr. Taylor's book "On the Art of Cutting
Metals." In this he shows photographs of the stages in
forging and sharpening metal cutting tools.[1]

Is it slavery to insist that a column of the same figures
shall always be added up to the same total?

It seems reasonable, for the greatest efficiency and
earning power, that each workman should be taught the

[1] See also "Bricklaying System," M. C. Clark & Co., Chicago, and
"Motion Study," D. Van Nostrand, New York.

exact prescribed motions that have been found to be the most productive, the least fatiguing, and the least wasteful. There is more to the benefits of teaching the exact motions than is commonly appreciated by the layman.

The advantage in speed, productivity, and ease of performance that come from habits of exactly the same sequence of motions and the absence of the mental process of making a complete decision for each motion cannot be appreciated by any one who has not made this subject a life study. The saving from this feature is a large one. For the best results, the best sequence of the best motions should be taught first, — taught and insisted upon until that sequence of those motions has become a fixed habit. Necessary and advisable deviations from this sequence will take care of themselves thereafter.

A book could be written on the *advantages of teaching the right motions before insisting upon perfection in the product manufactured.* In other words, Scientific Management insists that the novice shall use certain motions in a certain sequence until he can execute the work in the standard way, for the gains made by this process more than pay later for any cost of the time of the skilled worker going over and fixing up the first work of the unskilled worker. The ancient belief that a worker should do his work of *right quality of output first,* and fast afterward is wholly wrong. He should do his work with the *right motions first,* and either he or some one else should afterwards correct his work, or else throw it away, until he has formed habits of the correct motions. This method not only teaches him much quicker, but it also makes him much more efficient his whole lifetime.

I have never known a mechanic who had been taught the right motions who did not pity those who had not. Those who have only an academic knowledge of perspiration as a means of earning a livelihood should be comforted by the knowledge that the "slave of motion supervision" will have a pay envelope of much greater purchasing power to compensate him for his "slavery."

Does not Scientific Management "trammel the workman in the durable satisfactions of life"?

Not unless it is dissatisfying or unsatisfying to receive the best instruction obtainable and to do work in that method which time and experience have shown to be the least wasteful, the most productive, and the least fatiguing.

Furthermore, the working hours represent but about one half of the total time that the worker is awake. Under Scientific Management he has to work more regularly, and more constantly, but usually at not much greater speed. If this goes against his grain, it is more than compensated for by the greater amount of "durable satisfactions of life," as Dr. Eliot phrases it, that can be purchased with the excess money in the pay envelope earned under Scientific Management.

Why insist that men work separately instead of in gangs when, if they are in gangs, the best men will cause the slow and lazy men to work harder?

Experience proves that the output — when all men have their outputs measured separately — is much greater than when their collective outputs are measured as a gang.

Furthermore, the workers sooner or later argue to themselves in this wise, *i.e.* "What is the use of my working harder than any one else, since the results of my efforts are divided up among the gang?" Furthermore, a man realizes that, even if he rests considerably, it affects the average output of the entire gang very little proportionally, — and, as a matter of fact, the men do not make the lazy ones work. For an example of this see "Philosophy of Management," page 75.

In exactly what way can the men produce more output under Scientific Management?

In *Harper's*, February, 1911, page 433, Mr. William Dana Orcutt, after seeing the results of the installation of the Taylor System by Mr. Morris L. Cooke at the Plimpton Press, says: —

"Every task of the operative is preceded by preparatory coöperation on the part of his employer. When the order reaches him, every detail has been provided for: he has no questions to ask; the proper tools are placed beside him, and the materials themselves are near at hand. All his time is spent upon productive labor, and his output is proportionally increased."

PROMOTION

What show for promotion or development has a young man in a plant operated under Scientific Management?

Every show that there is, except pull. Pull might get the job for him; but he must have the merit, or the record of production and the unit cost records will show him up at his true value.

H. L. Gantt says, page 135 in "Work, Wages, and Profits ": —

"The development of skilled workmen by this method is sure and rapid, and wherever the method has been properly established, the problem of securing satisfactory help has been solved.

"During the past few years, while there has been so much talk about the 'growing inefficiency of labor,' I have repeatedly proved the value of this method in increasing its efficiency, and the fact that the system works automatically, when once thoroughly established, puts the possibility of training their own workmen within the reach of all manufacturers."

How can every man be sure that his merit will be discovered and that he will be promoted to the highest notch he can fill?

Because under Scientific Management the output of each man is recorded separately and the relative scores show up constantly.

High scores of output are accompanied by correspondingly high wages.

High scores and wages attract the attention of the management, which needs the services of teachers selected from those men who can make high records of outputs.

From the position of teacher the upward progress for the capable man is rapid.

Admitted that Scientific Management is better for most employees, what have you to offer to the successful all-around foreman under the traditional plan?

The "all-around" foreman, as his very name indicates, has to do many kinds of work, and to perform many different subdivisions of the several functions.

Not only is he in all probability much more efficient in some of his "all-around" duties than in others, but he is also using his valuable time in handling work that could be done by a lower-priced man.

Scientific Management offers such a foreman an opportunity to work constantly at his high-priced specialty. Thus he is more efficient, and we all enjoy that work most that we can do best. His earning power is also increased by putting him on high-class work on which he is most productive, and relieving him of ALL PAY-REDUCING DUTIES that could and should be done by a lower-priced man.

Further, he is taught the best methods that science can discover, — which raises him as a producer and earner above the earning power of his best work at his specialty.

Is it not a system of promotion based upon the contest principle — *i.e.* that the man who has the least regard for his fellows, coupled with the most ability, wins?

The traditional plan of management is sometimes based upon the contest principle; and so in a way is the Taylor plan, but under the Taylor plan, the winner does not win the loss of the loser, as he does under the old plan. On the contrary, the man even with the lowest score is paid unusually high wages, if he achieves his task, regardless of how much more some other worker may do. In other words, all may be winners under Scientific Management. It is not a case of *who* will get the prize by beating the others. It is a case of *how many* will get the prizes. For there are prizes for each and all that can be obtained by paying attention to business constantly.

Speed

At what speed does Taylor's plan expect any man to work?

At that speed which is the fastest at which he will be happy and at which he can thrive continuously.

Does Scientific Management permit speeding up in case two girls wish to race?

There is nothing in Scientific Management that would prevent two girls from racing if they chose to do so.   While Scientific Management does not encourage racing, it could not step in and stop any one from producing as much as he wished without being accused of desiring to limit the amount that could be earned in a day.

The quantity of output prophesied by time study as being the correct amount of output a worker should do in a day can invariably be exceeded by a spurt or a race.

One honest investigator was much disappointed by discovering that Scientific Management did not place a maximum on output of some women workers, — not realizing that such an occasional race to determine which was the smartest between girls who did not have time to enter athletic sports, gave them much pleasure as well as considerable extra money.   They had no fear of a subsequent cut in their rate.   Their racing record also proved that the set task based upon a high percentage of absolute rest for overcoming fatigue was so far below the record of race output that it was in no way unreasonable for everyday performance.

"Shortened hours combined with increased speed make the conditions of employment more favorable for high-grade labor and less favorable for low-grade labor. The better laborer does not dislike the speed and enjoys the time saved." — Arthur Twining Hadley in "Economics."

Do athletic contests between workers of different nationalities cause race feeling?

We have used the principle of the athletic contest for raising the efficiency of management for a quarter of a century.

Before and since we began the study of Scientific Management we have never seen any reason for criticism of the athletic contest. A periodical recently said that by means of putting different races against one another in atheletic contests, we created race hatred. On the contrary, we have never seen a case of race prejudice result from athletic contests, but we have often seen a keen interest and joy created by such contests. Furthermore, the workmen coming from the same country or district often have the same or similar methods of working, and much can be learned when two or more gangs with different methods are having a friendly contest against each other. The workers are given the pleasure of sport together with a day that passes quicker and brings higher earnings.

Does not the giving of a bonus to the foreman every time that a man earns a bonus result in the foreman driving the men unmercifully so that he can get the bonus offered to tempt his selfish interest?

No, because the task is set by carefully timing actual performance with the proper allowance of time for rest and unexpected delays. No driving is necessary after the workers have been taught the improved method devised by the best workers coöperating with the planning department. After the workers have learned the right improved method they will find it possible to do their task every day by simply working steadily without rushing. When this is not perfectly possible, the task has been set wrong and must be corrected without delay.

Does the practice of paying a bonus to the gang boss for each workman under him, and a double bonus to the gang boss for every day that every man in his gang earns his bonus, result in cruel driving of the worker, and abuse, discharge — in fact everything possible to coerce the worker into earning his bonus even on days when he is sick?

The "gang boss" gets one bonus for each time that the man under him gets a bonus, and a double bonus when every man under him earns his bonus. This makes the interests of the workmen and the gang boss identical. It makes them pull together. It causes the gang boss to do what he can to surround himself with the men who are best fitted by nature to do their allotted work. After these men have been selected, it is for the gang boss to protect and help them in every possible way to earn their unusually high wages, for he cannot get his otherwise. He uses all the brains he owns to help them from morning till night, regardless of how unsympathetic he may be by nature. He will spend no time scheming to get the old employees out and his friends and relatives in, for he realizes that the management has accurate measuring devices of the efficiency of the men under him and of him as an executive. He cannot bluff them. The facts will show up in their true condition in the unit cost column and on the chart showing fluctuations of outputs and individual earnings. The gang boss cannot discharge the workmen, for that is not his function. He will not recommend discharge for slight infractions, personal grudges, etc., because he realizes that to discharge a workman means to train a new one, — with a period when it is probable that at least one workman will not be able to earn his bonus. This means that during all that period the gang boss loses his double bonus plus the single bonus for the one or more men who did not make their bonus. Thus the gang boss thinks more than twice before he disturbs the usual daily working conditions.

Thus it will be seen that the effect of the single and double bonus on the gang boss is, in many ways, to make the employment of the employee more stable and permanent, and an incentive to conserve and use the special ability and efficiency of the trained worker. The gang boss cannot discharge or fine; and it is of no use to abuse the worker, for to recommend punishment that is not approved by the disciplinarian makes the gang boss ridiculous and subject to discipline himself.

Therefore the one thing left is to help the worker, — to help him to do his work, to achieve his task; to see that he gets his tools and materials without delay; and to see that the indication of hindrance or delay by breakdown is reported immediately to the repair boss, whose functions are to make inspections at stated intervals and to keep all machinery in the prescribed condition of repair so that breakdowns do not occur. Under the old scheme the gang boss usually "feels his oats." He abuses or ridicules, and is too busy to help the worker who is discouraged or is falling behind in his record of output.

Under Scientific Management it is better for the gang boss to risk ruin to his suit of clothes by jumping in and helping a man who is delayed by the happening of the unexpected than to let that one incident prevent him from earning the double bonus. Every time he thus helps himself he is helping the worker. There is no parallel to this under the traditional plan of management, except in the very small business where the employer is his own and only gang boss. This condition of scientific management has also many by-products of benefit to the workman. It fosters good feeling between the men and their employers. The men have more contented minds. They dare to push their work, knowing that when they really want help they can always get it. They soon learn to know that the gang boss is working for them, instead of their working for him. Their instructions are in writing on the instruction card. The gang boss can't change those instructions. If they work in accordance with the directions on the instruction card, the disciplinarian will stand by them. If they do not understand their instructions or cannot obey, they send for the gang boss. He is their coach, their tutor, and as the worker is paid more money for being more efficient, so also is the gang boss tutor paid in the form of bonuses and double bonuses in proportion as he is efficient as a teacher — not as a driver. The extra bonus offered to the worker is sufficient to induce him to put forth his best maintainable effort without the additional driving method of the "good old-fashioned" method of management.

UNIONS

Is not the real plan of Scientific Management to disband the unions?

The plan of Scientific Management in no way contemplates the disbanding of the unions.   In fact, all followers of Taylor recognize the general necessity for the existence of unions.   No one can study the subject of management without appreciating the good that has come as a result of the unions insisting upon more sanitary conditions of the shops and safer conditions of the buildings.   It is unfortunate that the unions have not always been right, but they have not.   Neither have the employers associations always been right.   The many times that each side has been wrong have been due to fear of injury in the future or revenge for real or fancied wrong in the past. But Scientific Management now provides accurate measuring methods and devices for determining the merit and efficiency of different methods of procedure, and the greater the accuracy of such measuring devices, the fewer the misunderstandings between the employer and employees.

The measuring devices find the facts and thus eliminate the largest part of the cause for labor disputes.   Mr. George Iles, in his intensely interesting and valuable book, "Inventors at Work," calls attention to the absolute dependence of advance in all sciences on the use of measuring devices.   It was the discovery and adaptation of the simple measuring methods and devices by Dr. Taylor that enabled him to make the greatest progress in the science of management and to eliminate war between the employer and labor unions.

These methods of measuring the relative efficiency of methods and men assist to eliminate industrial warfare. Instead of having war, the unions will recognize that under Scientific Management they obtain more money, shorter hours, fairer treatment, better teaching, and more sanitary conditions than their union asks from employers operating under the old-fashioned or traditional plan of management. There must always be unions; there must always be collective bargaining by the unions for some things; but the union that attempts to interfere by collective bargaining with the installation or progress of Scientific Management will, if unsuccessful, have its members left out in the cold, and, if successful in interfering with the management's installation, will so discourage the management that they will decide to postpone, for the time being or permanently, that one plan of management that will enable the workers to obtain unusually high wages. Neither the followers of Taylor, nor any one else, is able to install Scientific Management and simultaneously participate in a debating society or risk results of unfavorable decision of a well-meaning but uninformed board of arbitration.

I cannot emphasize too strongly to any and all labor unions that my advice is to offer no resistance whatever to any employer who is honestly trying to put in Dr. Taylor's plan of management.

After it has been put in and is in fairly smooth running order, the union men will find that their wages are much higher; that the hours are at least no longer — in fact are often shorter; that conditions are better from a health standpoint; and that, further, the square deal really does and must exist. Incompetents holding down positions due to graft, relationship, marriage, and "affinities," are measured up to their true value, and all can see this. The worker's job is sure, so long as he is efficient; the worker is reproved, disciplined, punished, laid off, or discharged by a trained disciplinarian and not by the whim of a suddenly exasperated gang boss, foreman, superintendent, or new manager. When the new manager handles this function of disciplining in any other way than with the square deal, then there is no longer Scientific Management.

This plan of Scientific Management extends and prolongs the years of productivity of the worker, not only because he is treated better, but also because it is entirely a teaching plan; and the old employee can teach for years after his usefulness would have ceased under the old plan of management.

There is no call for unions to cease or disband. If they do disband, it will be because they themselves decide that there is another way of obtaining a better result. The unions have nothing to fear from Scientific Management except that their own acts may unintentionally prevent its rapid installation.

If Scientific Management is a good thing for the workers, why do the labor leaders all oppose it?

They do not all oppose it. Some oppose it for the simple reason that they do not understand it; the others have visions that Scientific Management is something that will reduce the value of their jobs, — and all are afraid, because of the bad treatment that workmen as a whole have had in the past, that Scientific Management is simply a new "confidence game," presented in a more attractive manner than ever before. Because of the many cases of unfair treatment that the workmen have themselves experienced and have seen on every side, they simply cannot imagine Dr. Taylor or any other practical man working for their interests unless there is a " comeback " somewhere.

I have heard gentlemen considered well balanced in every other particular admit privately on one day that they knew nothing of the details of Scientific Management, and harangue a crowd on the following day telling of the evils of Scientific Management to the workingman.

As a matter of fact, there are but few men who, after having first become proficient mechanics in at least one trade, and after having been in direct responsible charge of engineering or mechanical construction, or manufacturing, for several years, can grasp in less than three to five years the fine points of Scientific Management that are necessary to make its operation successful.

Dr. Taylor and his followers, therefore, ask all those who do not understand this plan of management to suspend judgment not only until they understand it, but also until after they have had time and opportunity to talk to those mechanics and laborers who have worked and prospered under it for several years.

In this connection I would recommend for such interviews as typical examples of happy, loyal, intelligent,

well-treated, and well-paid workers, employees of the
Link-Belt Co., the James M. Dodge Co., and the Tabor
Company at Philadelphia.

Is it absolutely necessary to have no collective bargaining in order to install the Taylor System of Management?

No. But it will take longer if such bargaining is introduced. It would be like collective bargaining of the
doctors with all the patients in a hospital as to what
medicine Patient No. 40 should take.

WAGES

If the worker produces three times more output under Scientific Management than he does under the traditional plan, why does he not get three times as much wages?

If all of the saving by use of Scientific Management
were given to the worker, the management could not
afford to maintain the corps of investigators and teachers
who are necessary under Scientific Management. The
saving by means of better processes, easier conditions, and
more efficient teaching is so great, however, that increases
in wages of 25 to 100 per cent to the workman are always
paid. The balance of the saving goes to pay for the
cost of maintaining the conditions of Scientific Management and also for reducing costs of production.

In other words, the corps of investigators and teachers
is what enables the worker to achieve three or more
times the size of the output customary under the "good
old-fashioned" management. The savings caused thereby

must first pay for this corps, then the balance is divided between the employer and the employees.

What guarantee has the workman that the rate will never be cut?

There may be no guarantee to the workman that the rate will never be cut; but there will be no Scientific Management left if the rates are once cut, because the entire framework of Scientific Management hangs on first having the rate set by Scientific Methods and then never cutting the rate. Scientific Management represents the highest form of coöperation between the employee and the management. No management can expect any coöperation if the workmen have experienced a cutting of the rate with its after effects, namely, systematic soldiering. When the workers are caused by the cutting of a rate to figure out the greatest amount of output they can safely produce without another cut in their rate, there cannot be any further coöperation. Any one who has studied the subject of management enough to install Scientific Management will realize that the rates must be set right the first time and *never* cut. This is the best guarantee the worker can have.

What does the workman get if he exceeds the task?

That depends upon the method of payment that is used. Sometimes a higher piece rate for the entire number of pieces, as under Taylor's differential rate piece system; sometimes the same piece rate for all the additional pieces as the rate per piece of the task. If he exceeds the task much, he will be given a chance at the job of teacher or of gang boss, at either of which positions he can earn high wages.

Does not the management sometimes take advantage of the disciplinarian's power to fine the workmen and increase fines in times of business depression?

No, for the reason that under Scientific Management the fines collected go back into the pockets of the workman in some form or other.

Bitter strikes have occurred in many of the textile trades under the old plans of management, because the fines which were established primarily to compensate the employers for the injury caused by the employee were afterwards used as a means of reducing production costs, by the simple process of fining the workers for everything for which an excuse could be found.

Under Scientific Management the fines collected by the management for carelessness, disobedience, injury to machines or product are contributed to by the workers, gang bosses, functional foremen, and even those still higher up, at any time that the disciplinarian, in the exercise of his fair judgment, so decides. The money which is so collected is the nucleus of a sick benefit, insurance or entertainment fund, and is spent wholly upon the workers.

Such an arrangement offers no inducement to the manager or his disciplinarian to be unfair. The worker does not so much begrudge the money he has to pay, and every time the others hear of a fine being imposed they laugh in their sympathy, because they know the offender must pay and the management does not profit thereby. There is, therefore, no incentive for increasing fines in times of business depression, or at any other time. Then there is another benefit from the worker's standpoint. It is to the interests of the management to help the workers to do their work with the smallest amount of fines, because the management does not get the income from the fines, and any kind of fines, even necessary fines, cause some hard feeling. It puts the incentive on the management to remove the cause for fines.

What do you do with the bonus if the union refuses to allow the workman to accept it?

When the men refuse to accept high pay that has been offered to them, it should be deposited in a local savings bank subject to their order at any time. If they have earned the bonus that the management has promised them, then the management certainly should not keep it. Depositing it in the local savings bank shows good faith on the part of the management. When the worker gets old and helpless, he may change his mind and draw out his money.

CHAPTER V

RELATION TO OTHER LINES OF ACTIVITY

What can the colleges and schools do to help Scientific Management; or, what place have the colleges in Scientific Management?

This question is too large to attempt to answer in this book to the extent that it deserves. (See Bulletin #5, Carnegie Foundation, by Mr. Morris L. Cooke, M. A. S. M. E.)

There are five things, however, that would help tremendously: —

1. The colleges should arrange for the collection and interchange of time study data through a central bureau, preferably a national bureau at Washington.

2. They should establish laboratories for the study of methods for shortening the hours of the working day and for increasing the efficiency of the workman, foreman, and manager, that their earning powers may become greater.

3. They should study the reclassification of the trades, that they may be less wasteful and better suited to modern conditions. At the present time nearly all the trades are practiced to suit conditions now obsolete.

4. They should disseminate information and data regarding the economic benefits to the workers them-

selves, as well as the country at large, from having
everybody as efficient as possible and constantly producing as large outputs as possible *per unit of time consumed*,
so that honest men will not oppose labor-saving machinery
because of ignorance of facts.

5. They should disseminate the new method of teaching the trades, realizing: —

(*a*) That the best and fastest workman and the one
who can accomplish the greatest output with the least
fatigue is he who has been taught the right motions first,
speed second, and quality third;

(*b*) That the worker's accuracy at first should be
judged by his accuracy in conforming to the standard
method and not by the degree of accuracy of his resulting work;

(*c*) That this method is not a scheme for teaching slip-
shod results but, on the contrary, greater precision.
Habits of correct method will result in habits of correct
results.

How does Scientific Management affect the general welfare of the country?

Will Irwin says, page 949, *Century*, April, 1910: —

"To get the most out of a day's work and that without
injury to the workman's permanent powers, this is the
greater formula upon which the pioneers of the new régime
are working.   Carry the formula to its logical conclusion
and it embraces all those movements, formerly in the hands
of philanthropists and charitable organizations, which
seek to ameliorate working conditions.   As a matter of
self-interest, it incorporates the golden rule into the theory
of production."

What relation has Scientific Management to industrial education?

Scientific Management concurs with the new thought that ideal teaching in the school and college is but the putting of the student in condition to learn his real lessons, namely, those that he will learn out upon the work; and there is no end to these lessons.

Under the old plan the journeyman of each trade is supposed to teach the apprentice his trade. This method is an acknowledged failure, because there is more incentive to the journeyman to keep the apprentice from learning than there is to teach him. This is indirectly recognized by the unions in their laws governing more favored apprentices, such, for example, as the son of a member of the craft whom they know will have the best training that his father, at least, and perhaps his father's most intimate fellow-craftsmen, will give him.

The apprentice is taught so poorly and becomes efficient so slowly that he oftentimes becomes discouraged of ever learning his trade. These two conditions have in the past caused the term of apprenticeship to be five to seven years in England and America, and in the former country that is still the term in many trades. This length of apprenticeship is supposed to give the employer sufficient time to obtain enough profit from the boy's latter years to make up for his former years, when he was unskilled and wasted much material. In fact, the apprentice was so profitless that the master usually made him do other work, such as heavy labor outside his trade, chores about the master's house, errands, etc., in order to get some profit out of the apprentice during the first years of his apprenticeship.   The apprentice, obtaining little or no money for wages, in some cases going into debt to pay the employer to teach him his trade — his life work — was usually in constant trouble because he was not being taught as fast as he thought he should be, and was put to other unpleasant work, on the one hand, and was not working as hard as he should, on the other.   Under the best of the conditions, he was paid for his time and not for his output — was working on a " day work " basis with an agreed upon wage for a term of years without any definite agreed upon quantity of output that he should deliver in return. His teachers were of two kinds: those that did not care to teach him, and those that were not selected for their ability to teach, even if they were willing.   Furthermore, if they happened to be those that were willing and could teach, they taught what *in their opinion* was the best and most efficient method — without any help of modern methods of research and pedagogy.   Consider the stupendous waste of this method as compared with the method of teaching the trades under Scientific Management, where the teacher holds his position because of his measured efficiency to teach the one best way that science and coöperation have determined and selected.

It is here that the teachers in the trades schools will soon come into their own.   In the past they have suffered from a lack of the proper method of attack that made them become content with graduating boys who, with a little actual "experience" after graduation, could earn journeyman's wages.   These were, even then, looked upon as "incubator chickens." Now, with the method of attack furnished by motion study, time study, and exact methods and devices for measuring the ultimate subdivisions of mental and manual effort and fatigue, the teachers of our trades schools will soon be able to turn out "teachers of mechanics," that is, foremen; and the journeyman who does not learn his trade with the right motions first, and with all other recognized methods for the elimination of unnecessary waste, must take the place of him with the lesser skill.

The faithful old journeyman was a most inefficient worker at best — a less efficient teacher for lack of knowledge and incentive.

The best teacher of the present in the trades schools suffers in salary for lack of appreciation. The teacher of the future will be the best obtainable. He will be able to prove his efficiency by the measured quality of his output. This incentive for the teaching of the apprentice by specially trained teachers or functional foremen continues through the entire life of the worker. There is no end to the period of learning. Under Scientific Management a worker is better prepared each day to learn the new lessons that the investigators of the planning department have discovered or synthesized. The functional foremen and teachers of the management are better prepared each day to pass their information on. The appreciation of the merit of the best teachers of the trades in the future will carry with it an adequate financial compensation.

Is Scientific Management a factor in securing industrial peace?

Mr. William Dana Orcutt says, *Harper's*, February, 1911: —

"It has commonly been accepted that the interests of capital and labor ought to be identical yet, as a matter of fact, they have rarely been so considered.

"The new force, which is called 'Modern Scientific Management' says, 'If they are not identical, then make them so,' and having flung the banner bearing this slogan to the wind, it has thus separated itself from the systems and systematizing, from card indices, vertical filings, and cost tabulations. It recognizes all these as necessary details of system, which in turn is a necessary ingredient of Scientific Management — but as a science it concerns itself with cause and effect rather than with records or figures, which are usually obtained so late that they possess only historical value."

Is it not a scheme that will wedge apart the college man and the mechanic into opposed classes?

On the contrary, it is the one thing that will show the college-trained man and the young mechanic their interdependent relations. It furnishes an accurate measure of their relative importance. It shows them that for the best and most lasting efficient results they must work together and pull together; that each is absolutely necessary to the other in this plan of Scientific Management, not only during the period of transition from the traditional plan of management, but also after it has been installed and is on a permanent basis.

Does not Scientific Management remove the worker farther than ever from the management?

On the contrary, it brings him into closer touch with the management. He is treated as an individual and is not herded into a gang and treated always as one of a gang. He finds that by coöperating with the management in enforcing its system he raises his own wages, helps his fellow worker to earn more money, and helps the management to get lower production costs. This in turn helps his employer to compete successfully and therefore to secure more business, thus helping to prolong the employment of the workers.

NATIONAL INDUSTRIAL SUPREMACY

Would it not be better to nip the whole Scientific Management movement in the bud because of what will happen to us when the Chinese and Japanese, with their few requirements and low cost of living, discover and apply our methods of attack and laboratory methods as applied to the Science of Management?

Even if there were any force to this argument, it would be lost because it is now too late.

Native Asiatic engineers who have been educated in American colleges have already started the movement of giving their countries the benefits of Scientific Management.

How does Scientific Management affect reclassifying the trades?

First, its records show what parts of the work cause a lowering of the pay of the highly skilled man.

Second, Scientific Management endeavors to have each man so placed that he may work continuously on that kind of highest paying work that his skill, experience, and knowledge will permit him to do.

What place has Scientific Management in vocational guidance?

The preparation of the workman for his life work should begin while he is at school.

See "The Vocational Guidance of Youth," by Meyer Bloomfield, Director of the Vocation Bureau of Boston, lecturer on Vocational Guidance, Harvard University.

What place has so-called welfare work in Scientific Management?

The word "welfare" is usually disagreeable to the ears of the workers. Their viewpoint is that if there is any money to spare for welfare work they would rather have it distributed *pro rata* in their pay envelopes every Saturday night. Any kind of welfare work is better than nothing, and will help some; but to be permanent in its effect such work must be of a kind that enables the worker to be more efficient, to earn more wages, and thus take care of himself without any outside help.

The most beneficial "welfare work" would be the creation of a government bureau for the collection, preservation, and dissemination of data referring to Scientific Management.

Scientific Management hangs upon the science of time study. Dr. Taylor first called attention to the need of a book of time study data on the arts and trades, in 1895. There is not such a book on the market to-day, seventeen years later. Yet the government has employed experts to study how to increase the productivity of sheep, hens, cows, bees, pigs, and Rocky Mountain goats.

Who will be the man to receive the everlasting fame of being the first to start the movement for the permanent creation of a bureau and museum at Washington for the study of Scientific Management and methods of increasing the efficiency, longevity, and productivity of human beings?

Politicans recognize the great value of such a government department, but they are "vote shy." They fear the votes of a great number of workers who honestly believe that the sum total of "working opportunity," as they call it, is fixed and constant, and that to make one man more efficient and thus cause him to be able to do two men's work is simply displacing one more man to be added to the great army of the unemployed. The fact that this may be so this week blinds them to the fact that Scientific Management will quickly bring lasting benefits to them in the immediate future.

The case of the man who made the knitting machine for silk stockings in the time of Queen Elizabeth; the struggles to introduce the sewing machine, and the fountain trowel, and all the wars against the installation of labor-saving machinery since, are too well known to warrant writing about here. These improvements have come and are coming. Nothing can resist them permanently.

It is, however, a national, yes, a world calamity, that there are so many against any plan for saving labor. I am not able to see why, for example, certain unions insist, as did the bricklayers of Glens Falls, that outputs shall be limited by such crude methods as insisting that the bricklayer shall not lay down his trowel when he is picking up brick.   They insist that the bricklayer shall not pick up brick with both hands unless he also keeps the trowel in his hand.

I do not understand by what measuring device or method they have determined that that procedure is the exact one that is best for their craft.   If small outputs and long hours are desired, why not go the limit and say that no bricklayer shall have a trowel larger than the pie knife used in that vicinity, or that the wristband of the left shirt sleeve of each bricklayer shall be pinned to the leg of his trousers between the hours of eight to twelve and one to five?   This surely sounds ridiculous, but four hours of it daily would cut down outputs less than the other less noticeable rules of the Glens Falls bricklayers.

No friend of the working men can do his fellow man so much good as to teach the truth about the benefits to the workmen from increased outputs, — for increased outputs are the one thing, or condition, that will permit raising wages permanently and reducing production costs permanently.

The benefits to the workman from raising wages speaks for itself.   The benefits to the worker from reduced cost of production are not so obvious, but just as real, for when production costs are lowered the condition is made that creates greater "working opportunity."   Furthermore, reduced costs of production mean greater purchasing power of the wages of the workman, and reduced costs of living.

Scientific Management eliminates human waste as does nothing else.

Let us not be wasteful in earning money, even though

we may be wasteful in spending it for those things individually most desired.

"Give back the singing man!" and give him something to sing about and to sing with, and give him plenty of hours in which to sing, and furnish him with conditions during his work hours that will make him feel like singing after his day's work is done; and during the reduced number of working hours concentrate on how to eliminate human waste, unnecessary fatigue, and the workman's presence under working conditions any longer than is necessary to achieve the proper sized day's work.

INDEX

105

852168

Printed in Great Britain by
Amazon.co.uk, Ltd.,
Marston Gate.